More Praise for
# *Reading David*

"This book is a riveting and informative read. Lissa and David have laid bare not only the facts of dyslexia, but also the stark human emotions that lie beneath the label 'learning disabled.' I wish every teacher could read it and understand!" —Jane M. Healy, Ph.D.,
author of *Your Child's Growing Mind: A Guide to Brain Development and Learning from Birth to Adolescence*

"This is a lovely book. Every child with dyslexia should 'meet' David so he can help them through the diagnosis and treatment of this common problem. I and other adults who read this will want to take David home!" —Judith Rapoport, M.D.,
author of *The Boy Who Couldn't Stop Washing*

"A gripping story of a mother's discovery of her son's dyslexia and her efforts to help him. Parents trying to understand their child's learning disability will find this book a great comfort, not because it provides easy answers, but because it portrays the struggle so honestly. Wonderfully written by both the mother and son." —Ellen Winner,
professor of Psychology, Boston College,
author of *Gifted Children: Myths and Realities*

"*Reading David* turns developmental psychology into a fascinating, moving, enlightening, and personal story. It reads like a novel but teaches like a wise mentor. I recommend it for parents, children, teachers, students of psychology, special education, and life." —Dr. Georgia Witkin,
director of The Stress Program
and assistant professor of Psychiatry,
Mt. Sinai School of Medicine
and contributor, FOX News Channel

"Interesting . . . comprehensive." —*Tampa Tribune*

# Reading David

A Mother and Son's Journey Through
the Labyrinth of Dyslexia

*Lissa Weinstein, Ph.D.*

A PERIGEE BOOK

**P**

A Perigee Book
Published by The Berkley Publishing Group
A division of Penguin Group (USA) Inc.
375 Hudson Street
New York, New York 10014

ISBN: 0-399-53018-5

First edition: September 2003
Perigee trade paperback edition: September 2004

Library of Congress Cataloging-in-Publication Data

Weinstein, Lissa.
  Reading David : a mother and son's journey through the labyrinth of dyslexia / Lissa
Weinstein.—1st ed.
    p.  cm.
  ISBN 0-399-52934-9
  1. Dyslexic children—Education—Case studies.  2. Dyslexia—Case studies.
3. Special education—Parent participation—Case studies.  4. Siever, David.  I. Siever,
David.  II. Title.

LC4708.5.W45 2003
371.91'44—dc21

2003054718

*This book is dedicated to the memory of my mother,*
*Pauline Weinstein,*
*who knew that the mind of every child is fascinating.*

# Acknowledgments

When you write a book with your child, it's hard to know whom to thank. Do you thank the people who helped you, the ones who helped your child, or who helped the book? David felt I should dedicate the book to him, but I explained that you don't usually dedicate a book to your co-author. However, since it was my childhood dream to write a book and I doubt I ever would have dared without him, I guess he deserves credit for having given me my wish.

A tremendous thanks goes to my beloved husband Larry Siever, who has not only put up with me all these years, but was forced to read so many versions of this manuscript that the phrase "Till death do us part" must have seemed like something to look forward to. An even more special debt is owed to my younger son, Dan, whose kindness and deep good cheer has often brought us back from the abyss. He has always been a wonderful and adoring brother to David, and has generously forgiven my parental failings.

*Reading David* would not have been possible without Nancy Lederman, a true friend and a good writer, who offered bon mots, fine phrasing and a workable structure for our memories. My sister, Hillary Friedman has been there for me starting from the first day Pauline brought me home from the hospital, offering "good clothes in fine fabrics" when I most needed them, support at every turn and her invaluable sensible perspective. Don Davidoff and Betsy Lawrence also read earlier drafts and shared their knowledge.

Several people were helpful to David. Donald Cohen and Karen Guttman stand out in this regard. So do Pamela Miller, Helene Imber, and Jeanette Capshaw, all teachers who have the rare gift of being able to find something special in every child.

Thanks to my colleagues in the psychology department at City College for their admirable efforts to serve a neglected population in the schools in Harlem, for their friendship, and for intellectual companionship. A special thanks to Jeffrey Rosen for the pleasure of his generous insights into how brain functioning might affect psychological development. I'd also like to acknowledge my colleagues at the Pacella Parent-Infant Center of the New York Psychoanalytic Institute, who truly believe that every mother can become her own expert and to thank all the parents and children who have come to my office because I've learned so much from them.

A very heartfelt and special thanks goes to my agent, Marly Rusoff, without whom this book would never have left my file cabinet, for her faith and integrity, and to all the people at Perigee who helped with the production of *Reading David*: Sheila Curry Oakes, my excellent editor, her assistant Terri Hennesy and Shannon Sharpe.

"You're out of the woods, You're out of the dark, You're out of the night.
Step into the sun, Step into the light . . .
Hold on to your breath. Hold on to your heart. Hold on to your hope.
March up to the gate and bid it open."

Dorothy's entry into Oz
*The Wizard of Oz* (Warner Brothers, 1939)

# Contents

# Prologue

"How did the dinosaurs die out?" Sweating in the July heat, people waiting to enter the Museum of Natural History's *Jurassic Park* exhibit, turn to stare at the imperious two-and-a-half-year-old boy riding on his father's shoulders. David pauses long enough to check out a Tyrannosaurus Rex poised for the kill—short arms forward, powerful tail behind. For a magical second, the dinosaur seems to wait for David's answer to his own question. Imitating the way his father makes an important point, David holds his hands apart in the air. "Nobody *really* knows for sure," he shouts, chubby fingers splayed out with excitement as he senses the attention of his captive audience. David knows the theory that his Grandpa Ray, the geologist, told him. A comet hit the earth, the climate changed, and the plants died. He knows how the plant-eater dinosaurs starved and how the meat-eaters did, too, when they couldn't eat the plant-eaters anymore. He has a horde of small plastic dinosaurs collected from trips to the museum and walks to the Star Magic Toy Store. He knows all their names, arranges them into orderly lines, groups them by "type," or hides them in typical two-year-old play. He's concerned with how things disappear and where they really go when they are gone—part of his great struggle to understand the world and how he fits in it.

My husband, Larry, and I love the dinosaurs, too. Ferocious, guiltless predators. At age seven, Larry wrote his first book, carefully analyzing how the fish dinosaurs developed hard shells in order to protect, "those soft parts that were left out in the open." Now a biological psychiatrist, he's still struggling to understand the physical origins of the armor people use to guard their vulnerabilities. A psychoanalyst and child psychologist, I also probe the outcropping of primitive structures, scraping at metaphors and fossilized memories in the hope of finding clues to how we evolved.

We are experiencing a snapshot moment. I float for a minute above the crowd, seeing it all. The dinosaurs, the jeeps, the digging site, the admiring parents. We are thrilled. Could we really have produced something so amazing? David, our son, is exactly what we dreamed of, what we waited for—the best possible combination of us without any of our troubles. A clever son, a comical son, one who is not reticent to show himself. A son interested in the things we so value—ideas, science, facts, and intelligence.

**PART I**

The Wind Began to Switch:
Something Is Wrong, but What?

# Chapter 1

## The Problem

It's Open School Night. It's my first Open School Night because David is my first child and he is in kindergarten. Speeding home from work, no time to count change, I toss a random handful of coins into the tollbooth on the Henry Hudson Parkway. Full of purpose and determined to do it right, I join the long line of cars at the school waiting to park on the lawn. Volunteers direct us, waving flashlights against a thick fog rolling in off the Hudson River on this late September night. Still wearing my "Dr. Weinstein at work" uniform, I am sweating in tasteful gray wool and pearls. Rushing to be on time (7:30—Introduction with the principal; 7:45—Meet with classroom teachers; 8:15—Meet with specialists), I catch a high heel and sprawl into the sandbox. It's an inauspicious beginning.

The cornerstone near the entrance of the school announces the building's 1955 conception. A two-story redbrick structure built to withstand the Cold War, its functional, no-frills design and prominent American flag silently proclaim the down-to-earth values that are promoted here. The plentiful crimson leaves on the 300-year-old maple at the front offers further proof of the stability Larry and I sought in moving to this suburban town. Looking at the school, I'm sure we have made the right choice. David, still not even five, and Daniel, our

two-year-old, need never know the precocious maturity of city children. Here a child can grow up in his own time and not be afraid to
ride a bicycle in the street or walk alone.

Inside, the halls are brightly lit. The chipped paint on the doors
and window frames attest to the fact that sage green was a "hot" color
for fall at some earlier time. Above the bricks on the half-masonry
walls are bulletin boards filled with children's artwork and testimonials
("Why I love school," "My favorite place"). Room 111 . . . 109 . . .
Here it is, 103. Ms. Miller. Entering the room, I am immediately en-
veloped by familiar smells—open glue pots, nontoxic poster paint, fading construction paper, dried snot. Sitting dutifully in a chair that is
not the right size for this Goldilocks, I wonder which of the other
parents can be my friend.

To my left are cubbies where David hangs his new grown-up back-
pack, the one I worry is too big for him; near the windows is an area
for block building. Looking to see if any of the constructions saved to
show the parents belong to David, I find a drawing of stick figures
with the caption: "Me and my friends sitting around. We will share
our toys." Comforted by the complexity of the idea, I ignore how
primitive David's drawing is compared to the other kids'. Across the
front of the room hangs the obligatory string of cut-out alphabet letters
and numbers. At the kindergarten screening they said the school did
not expect children to know their letters yet. Teaching them that would
be the job of the kindergarten. I certainly haven't been able to teach
him.

David has dictated a note for me: "Dear Mom, Welcome to Open
School Night. I hope you have a good time."

I write back: "It was great to see your classroom and meet your
teacher. I know you will love being in school just like I always did."

Ms. Miller, an earnest twenty-two, sits on her desk, nervous legs
crossing and uncrossing beneath a long floral skirt. It's her first year.
She announces the class parents. I am one. She hands out materials on
how children learn letters and begin to read and write and explains
the kindergarten "curriculum." With tears in her eyes, she recites a
poem about the importance of play for children's creativity. She is
passionate, dedicated. I pat myself on the back again.

As I am about to leave, she stops me.

"I'd like you to go see . . . I'd like you to go talk with Mrs. Wilson, the speech therapist. I had her meet with some of the children in the class to evaluate their speech. The school has really good speech services. She's waiting for you now." She hesitates a moment, gauging what I can bear to hear, then adds, "It's very hard to understand what he's saying. I think it's frustrating for him."

Mrs. Wilson has written a report summarizing her time with David. Most of what she notes is expected, if not welcome, news. It *can* be very hard to understand what David says. Sometimes it's better when he's talking to people he is comfortable with and who are familiar with what he talks about. Mrs. Wilson found David's ability to replicate single sounds of speech, his "articulation," not *too* bad in isolation, although he consistently substituted the vowels "a" and "o" for the "l" and "r" sounds in sentences. His facial muscles are poorly coordinated, especially his lips and tongue. When he tries to put whole sentences together, he speaks so fast she found it hard to tell whether he was anxious or trying to use a vocabulary he couldn't pronounce.

What causes me to stare in horror is how David named pictures of common items, labeling a wagon as a "wheelbarrow," pajamas as a "nightgown," and a hairbrush as a "toothbrush." These errors were something different from troubling speech sounds. These were near misses, mistaken efforts to describe a picture that he recognizes but can't retrieve the exact name. I'd heard these funny things in his speech before, him using big words when little ones would do, like saying, "It's a *blustery* day" at age two and a half instead of, "It's raining." In my mind, I'd defined him as an unusual child with a huge vocabulary.

Looking at the words in print, I have the odd sensation of gears shifting. At that moment, I am somewhere else. The person reading the evaluation is not me, just someone who looks like me. It couldn't be me, because that would mean Mrs. Wilson is talking about my dear, funny, David, who is clearly not the person described on these pages.

Images intrude. The neonatologist, called into the birthing room during a difficult, long labor, taking tests of the scalp oxygen content to make sure "the baby" isn't anoxic. The fetal monitor of his heartbeat varying intensely with each contraction. The obstetrician saying upon hearing David's first cry, "That's the best sound you can ever hope to hear at a delivery." In memory, his voice sounds relieved. Was he worried? In doubt that there would be a first cry? I recall the seemingly benign diagnosis David gets the first night of "Transient Tachypnea," or temporary breathing problems. Was there a loss of oxygen to the brain? These facts are now rearranging themselves as realization dawns, and cruelly, that something is wrong.

Mrs. Wilson is waiting for my response.

"Will he read?" I ask, tentative, attempting a semblance of normalcy.

"Of course." Her voice sounds soothing, but the reassurance is hollow. I'm well aware that reading problems are correlated with language and articulation difficulties.

There are other, more deeply buried memories: a brain-damaged cousin left in my care while our parents are out. I poke at him because he won't speak clearly to me, his slurred words and his adamant refusal to leave his wheelchair is frightening and infuriating. My own febrile seizures in childhood, my mother's overly solicitous worry, her fear I am retarded like her brother's child. The images grow heavy, sticking together and then falling, forming a precipitate of guilt.

"If he was my son, I'd get him some help. There's a form you'll have to sign so I can do a more complete speech and language evaluation." Mrs. Wilson concludes our meeting. Another parent is waiting.

I take the form and the two-page summary, stuffing them in my bag and shuffling down the hall. Wandering aimlessly to the library, I meet a neighbor whose daughter is also starting kindergarten this fall.

"Lissa. Hi! What do you think? The school program seems really good."

A need to confess strikes as jealousy and embarrassment war within me. "They say David needs a speech evaluation. I . . . I don't want him to have any problems."

*Why isn't this happening to anyone else's kid?* I have the urge to lie, and I do.

"They think he's really very bright." (No one has even mentioned this.) A little white lie, like exaggerating my College Board scores by five points. A lie that couldn't mean anything to anyone, but betrays an underlying world of complex fantasies and imagined deficiencies beneath a calm surface.

My neighbor is a deeply kind woman. She ignores my statement or, more probably, is unaware of its significance to me and continues to chat. She's recently moved from New York City also and is thrilled to have her daughter in a public school. This moment is full of future to her. Suddenly, the fluorescent lights in the library seem too bright, and it's as foggy inside as out. My neighbor's voice is droning, far away and slow, a phonograph needle mistakenly left at 33 rpm. Segments of other conversations intrude:

"Ms. Lynch, the yeller. I hope Barbara doesn't . . ."

". . . not enough enrichment for the really bright kids. Sam should . . ."

Despite a growing sense of dread, I prolong the contact. I don't want to go home and see David's face. I can't imagine looking at him, knowing something about him that he himself doesn't know and couldn't understand.

## A Bear of Very Little Brain

When I was little, there were bright moments when everything seemed just perfect. After skating lessons, the blinding new snow frozen just enough for me to walk on top without sinking, or watching my mother, Pauline, taking out the baker's icing set to make butter cream flowers for my birthday cake. Working hard to solidify the image in memory, trying to block out less happy impressions, I would say over and over to myself, *You must always remember this. You must always remember this.*

I'm saying it now as I look at David, sensing that something precious between us is fast slipping away. He's waiting, staring at the birch we have called "David's tree," newly planted outside his window. Does he notice how thin, how frail it appears? David, too, seems vulnerable. He has always been an intense child, full of contradictions. Dark unruly hair; high, smart forehead; ears that stick out a little; large, mysterious, nearly black eyes. Sometimes those eyes are filled with radiance and excitement, but I've also seen them fog over with an inward glance that excludes others. Merry, impish. Funny words no one uses much anymore would be right for him. Not even Larry can make me laugh as loudly. Imaginative. But sad, too. David's lips are full but unformed; he tends to hold his mouth and jaws slack. His smile, when not completely comfortable, strains with the effort to get his face to match his feelings. His hands, I've recently noticed, are not strong. Elongated, weary fingers that never firmly grip but more often just hang in my own. He is wearing blue jeans, but I've had to do the snap for him, because he can't get his fingers around to close it himself. Buck-toothed and beautiful, he has a quiet, sly demeanor that appeals immediately to adults but not as easily to other children, with whom he is often shy. Sometimes, when no one is looking, he has a hang-dog stance. He is a child born to be rescued.

Always sensitive to my moods and anxieties, David suspects something is wrong. We do our most important talking in the car, when we don't have to look at each other.

"Mommy, is Winnie the Pooh a bear of very little brain? That's what they say about him isn't it? What does it mean to be of little brain?"

"I think that's what they say." Trying the psychotherapist's ploy of turning a difficult question back, I make a clumsy effort to avoid answering. "What do you think it means?"

"Well, I was wondering . . . Could you live without a brain? What would you be like with a little brain? How big is a brain usually anyway? What would you be able to do if you had no brain? Could you walk? Could you speak? Would something be funny about the way you talked? Could you remember things?"

He sounds excited; the pressure of his unvoiced thought—that he is broken—forces him to speak quickly. The rapid flow of the words signals an important idea, one that has to be released before it's forgotten or pushed aside. He needs to know the answers, but he's not just asking about anatomical realities, he's wondering about himself and, by implication, about me. How do I, his mother, feel about creatures with very little brains? For a moment I wish I didn't suspect the subtext of his question. How much easier not to see his pain and just plow on, doing the right thing, the thing that needs to be done. But his questions continue to come, thick and furious with worry.

"Why did they try to kill Wilbur?"

"You mean the pig in *Charlotte's Web*?"

"Yeah, that book with the spider. Did they want to kill him just because he was too small? That's not very fair. What does it mean to be the runt of the litter? What makes someone the runt of the litter? Can a kid be a runt, or just a pig?"

Could he really be asking if no one wants a child with problems?

## Nursery School

I don't remember too much about how I felt in nursery school. I had a best friend, Connell. I went to a nursery school where the mothers came in and worked every day, so you got to see your mother a lot. I remember we had a science teacher, Mary. She was great. I loved science. We would do these fun experiments every week. On Halloween she wore a big witch's hat and said she didn't feel like herself that day. It made us laugh. We had two regular teachers. One had yellow hair, and she would talk to me about bugs and fish. The other one had black skin, and she would hold me on her lap and talk to me if I cried. We had a turtle, Snapper. He looked at us. We baked cookies and grew butterflies and had imagination centers like a Japanese restaurant or a theater.

My teachers seemed excited by the things I wanted to know about like the early humans. We did a book with pictures of when we were one year old, two years old, three years old, and four. We had to say what we wanted to be when we grew up, and I told them that I wanted to be a scientist that studied dinosaur bones and early humans. I knew the word for someone who studied early humans—a paleontologist. My Grandpa Ray is a geologist, and he taught it to me. That was what I wanted to be, a paleontologist, but it was hard for me to say it. I didn't think anyone would understand and then they would say "What?" and I would have to explain. So I just said early humans.

The only thing I really hated about preschool was

swimming. I'd think, *Oh no, swim day again.* I hated going in the water. The water was too deep, and I thought I was going to drown. They made you slide down this big slide, and I was scared but I didn't want to cry in front of the other kids so I did it anyway. I couldn't tell how near it was to the water.

Sometimes I hated the playground because I couldn't recognize the kids. Well, I could recognize them. I just couldn't remember their names, so I couldn't call them. Even by the end of the year sometimes I still would forget their names. Like my best friend Connell had blond hair, but so did a boy named Teddy, but if they were running around in the playground, I would get confused about their names. I would try to tell them apart by their clothes, but if they wore the same color shirt I was lost. If I didn't play with Connell, I would stay by myself and make up stories. I liked nursery school 'cause I had a best friend. We would talk about our mothers and all the other kids. I never liked to go home with other kids without my mother being there. Sometimes, I would go home with Connell after I got to know his mother, Marthe, pretty good.

In nursery school we would have meetings on the big rug. They put the first letter of our names where we should sit on the rug. I didn't know what it was, but I listened very carefully when they told me where to sit. I made sure I sat in the same space every day. I listened carefully when they gave out the jobs because I couldn't recognize my name on the job cards. Connell knew all the letters in nursery school and he could write them. He told me it didn't matter that I couldn't find my name because he could always find it for me and write it on my pictures.

## Leaving New York

In the middle of nursery school, we moved out of New York City. Mommy and Dad were building a house, but it wasn't done yet. They sold our apartment and we had no-where to live, so we moved in with Grandpa Irv and Granny Pauline. Me and Mommy would take the train from that big station into New York City and then take a taxi to nursery school. Mommy would let me yell out the window of the cab. I loved going on the train with her. We would buy comics and she would read them. I sat on her lap.

Granny Pauline and Grandpa Irv were nice at first. Granny Pauline would read books to me every night. They wanted me to work on learning the letters. Grandpa Irv said I was being lazy. They thought I was stupid because I didn't want to look at the letters. Grandpa Irv gave me a typewriter. He said it would be fun for me and I would learn the letters that way. I just kept pressing all the keys different ways. He got mad and said I was fooling around. They wanted me to clean up my Legos, and Granny Pauline said I had too many toys and if I didn't have so many toys, I would have learned my letters. Everybody was try-ing to make me watch *Sesame Street* so I could learn the letters and numbers, but I hated it. It was for babies.

I can remember the whole downstairs floor of that house. I would have these weird dreams when we lived there. Black-and-white pictures of people screaming. I woke up once and thought *Oh my God.* I had another dream about a sad dragon and one with a boy with metal teeth and pimples.

Then Grandpa Irv got sick. Sometimes I hated him because he yelled at me and he never yelled at Dan, my little brother. He thought Dan was so cute. He would play games with him, but not with me. Once Dan accidentally knocked out the screen door. I was mad and I said, "How cute."

But when Grandpa Irv got sick and went up to his room and died a few weeks later, I started to get scared because I wished he'd die.

Then we moved to Irvington, and I thought it was

named after Grandpa Irv. I thought he might try to come and get me. I couldn't think about anything else, and moving to a town named after him scared me even more. We moved in September and I started kindergarten. I wasn't even five yet.

# Chapter 2

# Getting Tested

The speech lady (what *was* her name?) suggested a more detailed evaluation. Too suspicious to allow someone at school to evaluate David, I'm not willing to believe what I already know. A former colleague recommends Dr. Laura Tenzer, a highly regarded speech and language expert. Calling for an initial appointment, I use my married name, unable to identify myself as a doctor. In this context, I am just a mother. My professional expertise offers me no solace or special understanding. *How can I be a doctor and have a child with so many problems? I did all the right things, I studied hard, I didn't try to hurt anyone.*

In the car on the way to the doctor's office, I remember what I've told other parents to say to their kids about evaluations—keep it brief.

"We are going to see a Dr. Tenzer."

"Because of my speech?"

No secrets here. We had *never* spoken directly about his speech before and yet he knows immediately. I learn my first truth—David is already quite aware of his problems. I'm shocked. How long has he known that his speech is difficult to understand? How could I ever have believed he didn't know? Everyone was always saying, "What? What?" to him. Why couldn't I let him talk about it?

Dr. Tenzer and her staff are located in a suite in an office park, a group of buildings that cater mostly to business. A sign in the waiting room says "No eating or drinking." A placard by the receptionist reads, "MasterCard or Visa accepted." An industrial carpet is further evidence of no-nonsense efficiency. It's very different from the homey offices of psychologists in clinical practice, places designed to make you want to tell your secrets, places that offer Oriental rugs, comfort, and just a little dirt so you won't feel ashamed. I think of my own handwritten bills and haphazard accounting. No, this is much more medical, like the hospital clinics where I interned before retreating to the genteel world of psychoanalysis. This is science, a quantifiable wave of the future. It's intimidating and more than a bit alienating. But maybe they'll be able to fix things.

I glance at the other mothers in the waiting room. Silent women, faces tightly drawn, listlessly thumbing through children's magazines. Half of them are dressed for success, sporting laptops, flawless manicures, and busyness to differentiate themselves from their troubled children. The other half look like they are about to join the homeless— old running shoes, shapeless jeans, husband's T-shirts. A secret society of shame. No one wants to be here, to be seen here. It's a far cry from the happy chats in the obstetrician's office. Where are all the fathers?

Dr. Tenzer, an angular woman whose well-ironed navy-but-not-black style subliminally conveys professional competence, emerges effortlessly from the heavy door that separates the treatment rooms from the waiting area. *What do they do in there?*

After a firm, secure handshake, she asks, "Did you get the questionnaire I sent about his development?"

"I sent it back to you last week," I say, already guilty. She's probably better off without it. Filled out in my usual repentant style, it is covered with intense scrawling and asides. Asked if anyone in the family has needed psychotherapy in the past, I wrote "What psychoanalyst doesn't?"

Dr. Tenzer bends down to address David. "Is it okay for me to talk to Mommy alone for a few minutes?" David agrees, although it's unusual for him to let me leave him in new places.

Moving behind the door, I sneak surreptitious glances into the small treatment rooms. Each one is equipped with a young woman, a table, and two small chairs. Tools of the speech trade—peanut butter, Popsicle sticks, games, and stickers for good work. One larger space has rubber mats, huge exercise balls, a trampoline, and a trapeze. *I'm in the* Twilight Zone.

In her office, I summarize the issues and finally divulge that I am in the field and that we know many people in common.

On the way to get David from the waiting room, Dr. Tenzer asks, "Is it all right if I have some of my students watch through a one-way mirror?"

"Of course," I reply with slightly exaggerated grace, wanting to be seen as the cooperative mother, the one the professionals like. Secretly, I'm cringing. My son watched from behind a one-way mirror. What if they ask for a family meeting? Will we all have to come in and be observed? It's poetic justice, for all those years I sat in case conferences, secretly judging, believing I could have done better than another mother.

Lonely while David is working with Dr. Tenzer, I go over to Marsha, the receptionist, who stands stalwart between the therapists and all these distraught parents.

"The school thinks David has speech problems. I've always been able to understand him. Maybe he's shy. Do you think he could just be shy?"

Marsha gently interrupts, "I really don't know anything about him." She's understanding and must get a lot of this. I'm beyond any concern over making a fool of myself. I need reassurance. Like Picasso's *Weeping Woman,* I feel my face breaking up into its component parts, learning a new topography of pain.

David loves Dr. Tenzer immediately because she can understand his speech. She is also so skilled and knowledgeable about language that she manages to collect most of the information she needs without doing any formal testing. It's an art, her ability to connect with frightened children. After what seems like an eternity, she comes out and asks to see me in the office again.

"He's a thoughtful child, but he's sad about moving away from his friends in New York City. He loves to talk as soon as he feels someone will understand his speech, and he's not really that shy at all. He makes us all laugh."

These words are food. For a moment I feel safe, grateful that some-one sees my child as something other than a collection of problems. Dr. Tenzer says David will need to come a few more times. Someone else on her staff will evaluate his oromotor development. These are all new terms to me. Oromotor has to do with his ability to move the muscles in his mouth and to manage secretions like saliva. Dr. Tenzer says he has "low tone." *What is that?* She explains that it has to do with the development of the muscles and the signals they pick up from the motor neurons in the cortex. Low tone children tend to get tired and don't like physical activity. Dr. Tenzer suggests an occupational therapy evaluation. *Aha! The room with the rubber mats.* The only occupational therapy I know of is the "Let's make tile ashtrays"–type they do on the back wards of state hospitals, forcing patients who would rather sit and smoke cigarettes to do summer-camp arts and crafts. Is this what's in store for my David? David, who already had his college T-shirt purchased at his father's twenty-five-year reunion last year?

"I'm not sure what I'm seeing," Dr. Tenzer says in a brief meeting after the third session. "I think David's intelligence is way up there, but he doesn't have any of the usual skills kids need before they learn to read. He can only say the alphabet up to the letter F, and he can't count in order to ten. He can't recognize letters, not even the ones in his own name. Look . . ."

She writes *DAVD*. "I showed him this and asked him what was wrong. He pointed to the V shape and said it was the same as this one [the A] but that this one was upside down with a line through it. Anyone who is capable of making such an abstract visual analysis should be able to recognize letters. Is anyone in your family color-blind?"

"Not that I know of."

"Oh. He couldn't do any of the items on the Token Test."

The Token Test is a language test where the child has to follow instructions using a bunch of colored tokens (squares, circles, and tri-angles). Instructions range from "Touch the yellow circle" to more complex things like "Put the yellow square in front of the red circle." David seems unable to consistently identify even one color. Not being able to name colors and shapes is one predictor of future reading problems. Like letters, which are named arbitrarily, there is no reason that a square is called a square or red is called red and not yellow. Difficulty naming these arbitrarily named symbols will correlate with later problems learning letters and the letter sounds. Knowing that a written letter represents a sound is the basic process underlying the ability to translate the written symbols into words. The difficulty with naming shapes and colors also implied that David's problem with remembering people's names was not random error. Names are like letters, in that initially there is no reason that Al is Al and not Brandon or Zachary. It only makes sense after you know people, after they have a context in your life. If the world were conceived malevolently, the choices of names of things could seem downright capricious.

Dr. Tenzer wraps up. "I rarely suggest this for a child this young, but I know a developmental delay when I see one, and I don't think this is it. He should have a full neuropsychological examination. Dr. Prusser on my staff . . . ."

I interrupt before Dr. Tenzer can finish. "I supervised her."

"Oh . . . Well, how about Jane Neary?"

"I know she's the best, but we worked together at Mount Sinai. She's too close a friend. I . . . I don't want to burden her." I'm barely able to admit the true reason, even to myself, that I'm embarrassed by David's problems.

The recommendation for a full neuropsychological evaluation doesn't really surprise me. There are numerous signs of David's difficulties I've done my best to ignore, frantically overlooking what should have been obvious. Where David was concerned, I spoke only to people who would reassure me, people who would use the magic word *developmental,* a professional parlance for a problem the child will grow out of on his own, a mere wrinkle that will iron itself out in time, rather than a seam that will always stay visible. How blinding desire can be.

We settle on Dr. Martin. The people who do comprehensive evaluations tend to have waiting lists, so there will be a few months' delay.

## Speech Therapy

In the meantime, Dr. Tenzer recommends that David start speech therapy to improve the strength of his mouth muscles and occupational therapy to strengthen his torso. We are into the remediation routine so fast I can barely figure out what this will mean to David.

Dr. Tenzer cannot treat David herself in speech therapy. David had struck up a relationship with her and I imagined my professional ties should get David special treatment. Powerless to protect him even in the one area where I might have some pull, I feel at the mercy of strangers who will take over his care. Dr. Tenzer assures me the transfer to Korrina, a junior staff person, will be all right, and it is.

Korinna, a lissome beauty with the gentle aura of someone who has spent a lot of time meditating, bends to David on one knee, speaking softly. Although she is young, she intuitively understands his humiliation when he cannot do something. She never talks to me about him when he is present, knowing David finds it painful to hear his weaknesses exposed. She tries hard to find the right strategies for him, using his overall strong language skills and wish to understand how things work. They do games like blowing through straws, eating peanut butter, and chewing gum to strengthen David's muscles. Korrina gives him medals for good work, and he's proud of himself. David and I both fall deeply in love. Korrina is hope itself.

Sitting in the pizza parlor one afternoon, David says, "I had a really good day at school."

"David, did you hear what you said? You said 'school' not 'gool' like you used to."

"Wow. Gee thanks, Mommy. For telling me. That really makes me feel good."

*How little he needs to feel better. So far, no shame. So far, so good.*

Speech therapy is on Monday and Wednesday at 1 o'clock. I want to be the one to take David, but my professional schedule is tighter than the girdle suggested by my sadistic older sister when I turned thirteen. Realizing I *could* change my schedule is the first sign that the Red Sea can part, offering a surprising pathway to a new world. Alone during the day, David and I indulge our appetites at the office park cafeteria. In addition to the Gummy Bears and licorice we consume like criminals, there is time to talk and laugh, and for a little while, for a few hours at least, it is like before.

There is one thing we don't talk about. David never asks why it's so hard for him to speak like everyone else.

## Lemonopee

Before I went to nursery school, Mom and I used to go to this art and gym class at the 63rd Street Y. I really liked doing the art and climbing. At the end we would sit in a circle and sing songs. I would never sing. I couldn't remember the words, and I couldn't say them fast enough. Sometimes I would just move my mouth. I'd pretend or sing a little bit if I remembered. I do the same thing now if we have a recorder concert at school. I just make like I'm moving my fingers, but I don't blow in the recorder to make a sound. If I make a mistake, no one will know. The worst song ever was the alphabet song. I could never remember all the letters, or I'd say them in the wrong order. That part that goes L-M-N-O-P, I thought that was one word, like LEMONOPEE. All through nursery school we would have to sing the alphabet song. I still couldn't get it right, and to this day I always forget the letter U. Finally, Mom said at the end of kindergarten that it was over with the alphabet song. After kindergarten you never had to sing it again. Nobody would care if you could sing it. It was only a way of helping you learn the alphabet. By that time, I sort of knew the alphabet, but not always in order. I still don't like to alphabetize. But I was really happy that I wouldn't have to spend my life trying to sing it. Dan, my brother, is four and he can sing it, but I always make fun of him when he does. I tell him it's only for babies.

## Something Is Wrong

Overwhelmed with fear, I enlist as my ally Dr. Don Davidoff, a neuropsychologist and my best friend in graduate school. When Don met David at age four, I told him David didn't know his letters. With his usual precision, Don asked whether David didn't recognize the letters, or was the difficulty in writing them? Don said that if a bright child doesn't know the letters by four, it's worth looking into. If the child can't write the letters, it might be a motor skill problem, which is often (that magic word) *developmental*. I said I wasn't sure, but I knew he didn't recognize them.

Don and I review what I know so far. These conversations cheer me briefly because I'm pretending it's not David and that I'm discussing a "case" with my graduate students. I'm *really* good with someone else's child. Don suggests distinctions: the child who has a language-based problem that keeps him from remembering the letter names, or a child with a perceptual problem that makes the letters seem a little fuzzy so he can't hook them up with sounds. The perception problem is usually in the nature of a delay. This latter child might appear to start reading suddenly, as if he just "got it" one day, although a little later than his peers. I pray that this will be the case. We argue about whether David can recognize faces or if he seemed to get lost a lot in places he was familiar with like his school building. That would be a sign of a more general perceptual deficit, not one confined to the recognition of more abstract forms such as letters.

"Can he remember people's names?" Don asks.

"No."

"Does he get stuck on words?"

"Yes, but I think he covers it up because he likes to know different words that mean the same thing. It's hard to really pick it up in his speech."

"Can he follow directions?"

"I think so. Maybe. I'm not sure. I don't really ask him to do anything too complicated."

"Does he know the days of the week?"

"No . . . no to the names of the coins, no to the months in order, no to counting, no to the alphabet, no to singing songs. He hates to sing songs. *No, no, no, no!!!*"

"Lissa, it's okay. He's bright. I had this patient a few years ago—completely dyslexic. We worked on strategies to help him compensate. Now he's at MIT."

"Is it too late, Don? Is it too late?"

Don's voice exudes kindness. I see him through the phone lines, brows furrowed, thoughtfully rubbing his chin, picking up a hand to rest reassuring on my shoulder. He suspects what this means to me. He knows how long I waited to have children.

"No, Lis. It's too late when he's eight and already hates school. At five the brain is still plastic. C'mon, you know this. If you catch it young, you can help him before he knows anything is really wrong, before he's comparing himself to his friends and feeling dumb, before dumb becomes who he is and he stops looking at those words that make him feel stupid."

I am in the denial phase. I believe I can find someone who will make it go away. Despite Don's extraordinary tolerance, he finally says, "You have to wait and see what comes up."

*It's not his son. How can he know how it feels? He doesn't have children.*

## Being Read To

When I was little, really little, Mommy used to read to me all the time. It was my favorite thing to do. I would sit close to her, and she would put her arm around me when she read. I still want her to do that when we read. I liked the *Berenstain Bears* book, the one about "The Bad Dream." I had lots of favorites. I liked that William Steig book, *Rotten Island*, the one where all the creatures are hideous and love to fight. I drew my own Rotten Island creatures. I liked *The Amazing Bone.* The girl pig finds a talking bone who saves her life and they go on talking to each other forever. Mom's sister, Aunt Hillary, would send us cartons and cartons of books that cousin Joseph didn't want.

I really didn't like being in the playground when I was little. I liked to go to Central Park and sit on the grass with Mommy or Carole, our baby-sitter. They would read to me all afternoon. Carole said that she had never seen a kid who liked books as much as me. It was a joke in the family. Once when I was really upset, I said, "A book, a bookie will calm me down," and everyone laughed. Mommy used to read to me for hours. But now looking at books just makes me sad. Everyone says, "You should try to read. You'll like to read." Why would anyone want to read? What is so great about reading? Mommy can always read to me.

## Full Neuropsychological Evaluation

**Day One:** 8:30 in the morning, an Indian summer morning in late October. Today, David begins his "full neuropsychological evaluation," an uncommon occurrence in the life of a five-year-old. We have to hurry. We have an appointment at a hospital in Queens, a distance from our home. I grew up in Queens, but I don't know the way there in the car and I could get lost. I'm sure to get lost this time, because I don't want to go. I'm afraid.

I'm dressed well, if a little too warmly, following my mother's edict that it is important to look nice when you go to the doctor or dentist. The heat of the autumn sun doesn't reach me. Larry goes in another car. He will return to work after we speak to the doctor.

The evaluation will involve ten hours of testing. There will be an overall test of intelligence, additional tests of pre-reading skills (such as letter and number knowledge), tests of large motor skills (balance, strength, and the ability to plan a sequence of activities), and fine motor skills (such as drawing and writing). How David hears and produces language will also be examined, as well as his perceptual abilities, memory, and visual and verbal attention. The doctor we will see is an old teacher of mine, one of the original researchers on reading problems in children, but I didn't pick him for his expertise. His friendly voice on the phone made me feel that he would protect my David from harm. I've told David we will see a doctor who will help find the best way for him to learn.

The way I'm rushing, you would think being late would change the results. We drive past the familiar wide streets: Astoria Boulevard, Grand Central Parkway, and Queens Boulevard, home of the old Alexander's department store. These were my streets of adolescent possibility, where I rode with boys who had just got their licenses and, trying to look tough, pretended they had stolen their older brother's car.

We do get lost, but just a little. David is telling me about the letters, or maybe, in my apprehension, I've asked him something. I've become the Grand Inquisitor, trying now to unearth the information I'd worked to keep hidden. He seems to like talking to me less and less.

"At first the letters just looked like squiggles. I couldn't recognize them," he says, trying to be helpful. "Then I could recognize them. I can see them now. I know I've seen them before, but I still don't know their names. Who named those letters, anyway?"

It's a good question, one I don't know the answer to.

We arrive at the doctor's office. It's an old building with the look of a genteel mental hospital past its prime, where people sent relatives who suffered syphilitic degeneration or tried to hide the ravages of tuberculosis. Larry meets us at the door. We go in to talk to Dr. Martin. He is older and heavier, more officious now that he shed the jeans and sneakers of his assistant professor days. It's obvious immediately that he doesn't remember me. Why should he? But still, I'm insulted. *Can he really take good care of David?*

He has an "assistant," a less-experienced graduate student who will actually administer the tests. I had forgotten that, as part of his training program, Dr. Martin lets students do the work while he supervises the interpretation of the data. *Oh great. Some neophyte will test my son.* Already mistrustful, I'm silently making a list of everything he's doing wrong, just in case I don't like what he says. And we haven't even begun yet.

Larry and I talk briefly with Dr. Martin to orient him to the areas of difficulty. He is reassuring, saying that boys often experience delays in learning their letters. It's not serious if nothing else is wrong. I think that's what he said. Maybe that's not what he actually said. Maybe he wasn't trying to be reassuring at all. I have started to listen selectively in accordance with what I want to hear.

While we talk, David is copying letters from a speech medal Korrina has given him.

"That's interesting," Dr. Martin comments. "Kids with problems with letters don't usually do that. They try to avoid the letters."

The medal says "GREAT WORK."

*See, everything will be all right. He said kids with reading problems don't like the letters. Dr. Tenzer was wrong. You need to see someone with the right experience to know what's going on. Everything is fine. I knew it.*

Larry leaves. David and Dr. Martin begin the testing. I sit in the hallway. The walls, once a robin's-egg-blue have faded to gray. The place could use a little cheering up, maybe a fresher color on the benches. Suddenly, I'm the Martha Stewart of institutional décor.

Psychology interns walk the halls, filled with the importance of their new "near doctor" identity. That was me fifteen years ago. But I am on the other side of the table now. I'm a patient. Worse, I'm the mother of a patient. Interns always try hard not to stare at you. That would be unprofessional. But it's clear that you're here, waiting. No one is waiting for good news.

I've brought work with me. Work protects me from being just another mother. See, me, too! I'm a doctor! I bring the results of a series of tests that I am doing on an eight-year-old child. I am scoring and writing my evaluation of another child, in what seems like another world, while my child is undergoing the same thing here in this . . . hospital. Nothing gets done.

After what seems like an eternity, Dr. Martin comes out. "Your son is anomic," he announces with ill-disguised pride. He is quite cheerful, excited that he's understood something. *Does he think this is good news?*

He continues. "That's why he can't name the letters. He uses low-frequency words to defend against the high-frequency words he can't remember. We can still teach him to read pretty well—if there's nothing else."

The doctor's enthusiasm is unsettling, but all too familiar. I've had it myself. It's an intellectual pleasure. You're doing detective work, and you've read the clues correctly. When it is somebody else's child, the whole evaluation procedure is a fascinating puzzle.

*God, what a pompous ass. Look at him. He's so pleased with himself, all puffed up with what he knows.* From the other side of the table, that mother side of the table, intellectual enthusiasm looks like cruelty.

Pompous or not, Dr. Martin is not the school speech pathologist. He's a world-renowned expert. If he says there's something there, it can't be easily disavowed. What David has is not nothing. It's *anomia*. Not that calling it anomia (which is just another word for difficulty in quickly recalling the names for things you already know) gave us much new information. After all, David had told us he had trouble naming the letters. Like so much of the arcane language in psychological and psychiatric reports, rewording masquerades as knowledge, functioning to make professionals feel special. Suddenly I understand what parents mean when they come to my office and say they've had their children tested but can't understand the results.

There *is* one thing new about calling what's wrong with David *anomia*. Now the problem has an official name and that name means *trouble*.

In the hospital's overheated institutional cafeteria, red Jell-O squares stare from their pastel melamine plates. Tensile, rubbery hot dogs bathe in the stale smell of steam from warming trays.

"David, drink some milk." At least I can feed him the right food.

"I can't Mommy. It makes me sick. It's sour."

Driving home through the Bronx, we stop at Toys "Я" Us and buy a humongous toy. It's a Mighty Max extravaganza—Skull Mountain. A series of dangers take place in a menacing skull. Our miniature hero, Mighty, *will* overcome them. Maybe a toy will fix the pain. We will try anything. Maybe a toy will help David feel for a moment that the special something is not missing, something intangible but so necessary, something whose name changes. Now you've got it. . . . Mommy's love, Mommy feels you're perfect. A perfect body, a perfect mind—you have everything.

**Day Two:** We return a few days later. Dr. Martin explains that they are getting to the stuff that is hard for David, the "motor" stuff that will assess his ability to plan and execute a series of physical movements, his balance, ability to hop, or hold a physical position. These tests will tell how he will perform in those "boy" activities so popular in the suburbs, baseball and soccer.

David takes his Skull Mountain with him. During the ever more frequent breaks he needs to get away from the testing, he plays with his toy. Mighty Max is in real danger.

"Watch out Mighty. Here comes the Evil Eye. You can't escape. *Pssh!* Poison spitting out. Look, Max is getting crushed in the elevator. Aargh! He can't walk. He's falling. He's falling again. Mighty's going to be killed this time."

It doesn't look good for the hero in this game.

David and I take a lunch break at Burger King. The free toy is no good, the food is "yuck," and we have to park too far away. Our conversation is stilted, different from our usual "seeing the world the same way."

"Is it fun for you with Dr. Martin?"

"Not so much, not really. Sharon [Dr. Martin's assistant] doesn't understand anything I say so I don't say too much."

"It's not fun at all?"

"Well, maybe just a little. Could we get a toy on the way home?"

"We got one yesterday."

"Couldn't we get another one?"

I know the tests he is getting. One of them is the Weschler Test of Preschool and Primary Intelligence (WPPSI). It's a compilation of ten different subtests, each of which measures a different component of intelligence. The subtests measure perceptual skills, the ability to recognize what's missing from drawn pictures of common items, logical thinking through the ability to form verbal abstract categories, spatial and constructional skills through the ability to analyze and reproduce abstract geometric patterns with blocks, the child's fund of information, and how well they understand the rules of the world. I've taught the Weschler to my graduate students and given it a hundred times myself. A child's vocabulary is a good general measure of their intelligence. I'm a vulture, quizzing David on his responses, desperate to know the scores:

"When you were telling Dr. Martin what the different words meant, what was the last word you did?"

David, sensitive to any possible shortcomings, does not answer. Thankfully, lunch is over.

On the way back to Westchester, I drive through my old neighborhood, a virtual desert of shabby discount stores and gas stations, built in full auditory proximity to La Guardia Airport. At sixteen, I vowed to leave forever, hastening my exit with the blessings of higher education. Who said you can't go home again?

## Doing All These Things with All These People

We went to Dr. Martin five or ten times. I remember Sharon. What did Dr. Martin do when Sharon tested me? I didn't do anything with Dr. Martin. I was with Sharon. There was some stuff I didn't want to do and some stuff I couldn't do because it was too hard. I remember that once we went under the table to play a fish game where we matched the letters with something. I couldn't do that and she kept yelling at me to do it. It didn't sound like she understood me when I talked to her. She kept saying, "What?" I wanted to make a bar, and she kept saying, "A bore? A baw?" I didn't get why she couldn't hear. The word sounded clear to me. So I just said I wanted to make a table. I knew she could understand that. After a while I didn't want to talk to her anymore. I'd get angry when she didn't understand me and mad at myself. It made me sad. I thought no one could understand me. We didn't do any blocks. Maybe I told her what words meant. I didn't like her. I thought she was a devil. Not really. Just kidding. I thought of her as one of those girls who was a kind of nice but snotty person. She made you do things you didn't want to do. I don't remember.

It was a long drive. I didn't know why we were going.

We did do block-balancing things. Or maybe I did that with someone from Dr. Tenzer's office. I remember they had a cafeteria at Dr. Martin's, but the food was just horrible. I had milk. Mommy made me have it, but it tasted horrible. We got a big toy at the end. The next day we went to visit Connell, and I gave him the toy. I didn't want it anymore.

I remember going with Dr. Tenzer. I liked her a lot. She was very nice. She liked Legos a lot. She was a very nice person. I went with a group of ladies who made me try to make sounds. It was weird. All the ladies kept telling me to try.

Why were we doing all these things with all those different people? Because you were making me. Well it was hard. I couldn't do hardly anything.

## Waiting

Sitting with Marthe, Connell's mother, in their comfortable, homey West Side apartment, so familiar and safe, for a moment I can believe David would be fine if we hadn't left New York. Marthe and I talk in secretive whispers, pretending that David can't hear. I know it's not true. Children have ways of finding out every secret.

"He's not going to read, Marthe."

"He's so bright. He's just like Connell. He'll find his way."

*Who can trust Marthe? Connell tested in the ninety-ninth percentile. He knew his letters in preschool. Well, he has problems, too. He won't share. He's not perfect.*

What is happening to me? I've always loved Connell—from the moment he became David's best friend in gym class at age three. I see a long spell of loneliness and a complete absence of humor. "Will David be all right?" "Do you think he'll be all right?" torturing my friends with questions, the same questions, over and over. I talk to strangers, revealing secrets in the hope of feeling nothing. Reassurances offer only momentary respite. Talking, talking, talking . . . My fingers

curl tightly, my teeth will shatter against each other from biting down.
No one can stand me anymore.

Even my ever-patient sister loses her temper.

"They all have problems," says Hillary practically. "What if he
were dying? Would you care if he couldn't read?" Then she delivers
the clincher, with the deadly aim of an older sister, "God, you're just
like Mommy. Nothing is ever perfect enough for you."

*Not read? David won't read? How can anyone survive childhood
without reading?*

Library day was the most important day of my whole week when
I was a little girl.

### A Trip to the Library

*The library is the biggest building on Main Street, Flushing, on
the same side as the synagogue and the flower store that grows
the baby chicks at Easter who claw out of their shells and step
on each other's heads, across from the home for the nuns who
waddle together in long penguin outfits.*

*When you go in through the first set of doors, there is an
auditorium on the right. Hillary goes to talks there with
Mommy that I am too young to hear, talks with titles like
"Growing Up and Liking It." Afterward, Hillary comes home
with books with pictures of sweet potatoes with arms growing
out of them that end in wiggly fingers and say "Fallopian
tubes" underneath. I don't know exactly what those are yet,
but I know you can learn it in a book.*

*More double doors get you to the desk for choices where
the lady with glasses puts in her smudgy dates. Behind the desk
are adult books, and to the back is the room with encyclopedias
and books on witchcraft and presidents. Upstairs, up the
curved pink staircase which Cinderella could have walked
down on her way to the ball and is not straight like the stairs
in our building, are the children's books.*

*I am working my way through the Dewey decimal system
category by category. I know I will read every book in the
library some day. I have already learned about boys who mea-*

*sured Arabian stallions with their hands, pirate girls who don't care how they are dressed when they climb rope ladders and look far, and Marie Curie. She and Pierre, her new husband, trade their wedding present for bicycles. They don't care about money. Soon, they will burn their fingers and discover radium.*

*After we choose, Mommy lets us sit in the garden. It is only cement enclosed by high walls that shut out traffic noise, but I know it is the courtyard of the king, ugly from the outside in order to hide a jeweled world that only those allowed in see. I clutch my books to my chest, watching the shadows of other children playing hopscotch. I know I don't belong here. My real parents are like the people I've met in the books—queens or race car drivers or scientists. At night, I don't hear Mommy and Daddy argue. I am reading.*

# Chapter 3

# The Problem Has a Name

Six weeks later, we're back at the hospital. In true psychiatric style, Dr. Martin sits across from us behind a large desk with a busy calendar blotter in his sun-filled office. Confident of his findings, he glances only briefly at the results, having done these "informing" sessions hundreds of times. Pictures of his own successful children stare at me. They are older and seem to have already triumphed over educational adversity. Dr. Martin speaks in a soothing voice, full of his own knowledge. I sit with yellow pad in hand, taking dictation. Years ago, working as secretary, I learned you can take down all the words without having to think about what is said.

Dr. Martin addresses Larry. They are powerful, smart, men, and they talk in a chummy and collegial way about things like localizing the areas of damage in the brain . . . Terms like *basal ganglia* and *angular gyrus* float in the air.

An instant replay of my amniocentesis flashes in my memory. Spread-eagle on the gynecologist's table, naked from the waist down, my obstetrician and Larry discuss the differences between vaginal ultrasound and regular ultrasound as he moves the monitor across my belly. My beloved obstetrician, on whom I have developed such a crush that I am considering asking him to father my second child, is talking to Larry, not me. "Hey, it's my body! My baby. Can someone talk *to* me, not *over* me?"

Here we are again. Big docs! Talking to each other, even when I know more about the meanings of these findings than Larry. Are mothers considered stupid by definition?

"What causes these things?" Larry asks, hoping to allay my obsession with my culpability.

"It's hard to say. Most often these things happen during the birth. They've been doing studies."

I don't hear the rest. Remembering my prolonged labor, the cord around David's neck. Rage washes over me—toward my obstetrician for not sectioning me, toward Larry for not insisting we go to the hospital when the contractions did not progress. Then the blame shifts to me. It is my fault; my body, the betrayer has done this. Old ghosts linger in the shadows created by David's difficulty.

"Why did this happen?" Behind this perfectly reasonable question is always a fantasy. I've heard a million guilty imaginings in my office. A mother feels she had done something during the pregnancy ("I drank a little," "I worked in a lab with toxic chemicals") or perhaps she wasn't "really sure I wanted a child" or maybe it was her fault because of genetics ("I had a little trouble reading," "My father could never pay attention"). Maybe the obstetrician didn't do something ("If only I had been sectioned, but I went to an obstetrician who didn't believe in sectioning"). Maybe it's her husband's fault. The list is endless and as individual as the mothers who bring their children for help. Not one can submit to the randomness of fate.

Larry and Dr. Martin continue talking. Now it's about the insurance company and how to get this paid for.

"*Excuse me*. What do I do now?" the hollow stridence behind my words surprises all of us.

Dr. Martin lays out a sensible program. David should continue in speech therapy with Korrina, whom he trusts. In the context of speech therapy he can be taught the letter sound associations, which are the basis for reading, by learning the feeling in his lips and mouth as he says the letters. The physical cues will provide an additional set of associations to the usual auditory and visual cues. Although David seemed aware of and tried to hide what he couldn't do, Dr. Martin thought any depression might be a realistic reaction to seeing that he cannot do what his peers accomplish easily. Therefore, he didn't recommend psychotherapy because so much intervention would increase David's sense of being flawed.

"Is this a threshold problem, or will he always have trouble learning to read?" I ask. There is a significant difference between children who have trouble learning the "code" of reading—learning to translate the written letters into sounds—and children who have trouble with the structure of the language so they have difficulty with both listening and reading comprehension. The former problem looks a lot worse in the beginning but is actually less dire.

"Once he learns to read, he should go on to read at the level of his vocabulary and comprehension, which is pretty good," Dr. Martin replies.

Okay. But myriad pieces of this puzzle remain unsolved. How hard will it be to teach David to read? How much will the difficulty and slowness of his reading affect his understanding of what he reads? I cling to the illusion that all I have to do is teach David the letter sounds and he'll be able to put them together. But it's really not so simple, because the same underlying problem that causes him to have trouble naming isolated letters will also retard his ability to identify whole words, even after he knows the individual letters.

Good-bye travel soccer team, good-bye Rhodes scholarship. In one minute David has gone from being someone "normal" to someone who is on the treadmill of developmental difficulty, a child whose pleasure will be bounded by the schedule of his remediation, of his need for help.

Peeking over at Dr. Martin's folder, I see the IQ scores. They are lower than I would have predicted, placing David in the average range of intelligence, not above. Trained in psychological testing, those numbers still seem sacred to me, now they are more a life sentence for my son than a diagnosis. Tears form and twitches escape while I say, "It's very sad; he's very special." Dr. Martin and his assistant Sharon nod, smiling, the way they have nodded one thousand times before to parents who cannot give up the idea that their children are unique. It is a TV smile—seemingly sincere, but empty.

Back on the Major Deegan highway, I am hypnotized by the rhythmic choreography of cars changing lanes. Memories scroll by, but in reverse order, like those calendars in old movies where the dates blow backward in the wind. David's thrill at pedaling his tricycle, the confused "Is this me?" look on his face after his first halting steps, his reassuring ability to take the breast right after birth generously quelling my doubts that I could be a mother, Larry and me in the taxi on the way to the hospital, the phone call telling Larry I was pregnant, the diminutive rabbi at our wedding stretching up to reach our foreheads, saying we must be sure to take time away from our careers to be together, our first date spent smoking delinquent cigarettes in the joyous disobedience of new love. Now the scene gets smaller and smaller, a picture on a TV tube, until it is no more than a white dot and *blip!* It is gone and none of this ever would have happened.

## 315.39 Phonological Disorder

The next few weeks are spent reviewing what I believe to be Dr. Martin's flaws. He used a trainee; he didn't do the testing himself; he wasn't explicit enough about the processing issues; he didn't try to understand David's speech. Why do I really hate him? Because he is the one who put a name to the bad news; he's the one who verified that the problem was not developmental and that it would be lifelong. I hide the notes from the meeting under the place mats at the very bottom of the kitchen cupboard, hoping to protect us from their black magic.

The notes say that David has to suffer through the relative unintelligibility of his speech, which makes it necessary to consciously monitor activities that most people do automatically. Even though he has a good vocabulary, his speech problems force him to choose a word that he can pronounce well enough for other people to understand. The notes say David has a hard time quickly retrieving the exact word he wants and that he has not acquired stable shape and color names. Children with these problems have trouble learning to read.

The notes say David is hypotonic and might tire out more easily than other kids. Sequential motor activities like jumping jacks, riding a bike, or handwriting will be hard for him, and he might have trouble stopping a repetitive activity (like running fast) once he's started. For these reasons, sports will bring him little pleasure. The notes say David tries to protect himself from shame and to avoid things he believes he can't do.

At the bottom of my notes are diagnoses. Now the problem has a name and it even has a number, several numbers from the revered Diagnostic and Statistical manual, the DSM IV, the bible of psychiatric nomenclature that groups collections of identifiable symptoms into diagnoses. Larry had worked on the DSM IV, heading one of the research laboratories in personality disorders.

Poetic justice. All our professional lives, Larry and I have given out these numbers. Not cruelly; it was part of our work, a summary of our findings, a way to expedite insurance coverage. *Did we say to ourselves "Not me, not my child?"* Now our son, our David has one. Now I can't block out the whole life behind every number. Every digit is someone's broken dream.

315.39 Phonological Disorder: a consistent failure to make correct articulation of speech sounds at the developmentally appropriate age. When David reaches the age where his ability to read can be tested, he will also be 315.00: Developmental Reading Disorder and maybe 315.80: Developmental Expressive Writing Disorder.

I consider briefly some numbers for myself. First choice: 296.2 Major Depressive Disorder, single episode. Soon to come, the inevitable V61.20: Parent Child Problem.

### *Dys* (Difficulty) *Lexicos* (Pertaining to Words)

When the going gets tough, I go to the library, into the stacks to comb the literature for a way to "fix" it. I find *lots* of books on learning disabilities: scholarly books on child evaluation, books attempting to translate the secret and archaic language of psychological testing, books on how to diagnose learning problems, books on how to deal with schools, books on how to do cognitive remediation, books on the processes involved in reading. Here are the basics:

Dyslexia is an unexpected difficulty in learning to read or spell that is not due to poor schooling, a peripheral sensory handicap like blindness or deafness, acquired brain injury, or overall low intelligence or low socioeconomic status. These exclusionary conditions might affect reading, but by themselves, they result in what is known as "garden variety poor readers" rather than dyslexia or specific reading disability. However, dyslexia might contribute to low IQ scores or result in low socioeconomic status, as the child's failure to read might affect his capacity to acquire information and concepts or to succeed in the school system or job world.

The current official definition by the National Institute of Child Health is:

> "... one of several distinct learning disabilities. It is a specific language based disorder of constitutional origin, characterized by difficulties in single word decoding, usually reflecting insufficient phonological processing abilities. These difficulties in single word decoding are often unexpected in relation to age and other cognitive and academic abilities; they are not the result of generalized developmental disability or sensory impairment. Dyslexia is manifested by variable difficulty with different forms of language, often including, in addition to reading problems, a conspicuous problem with acquiring proficiency in writing and spelling." (Lyons, 1996,34)

Whew! There are a lot of words in that definition. I break it down, point by point:

**One of several distinct learning disabilities:** Dyslexia is not the only learning disability. It is, however, the best researched and the most common neurobehavioral disorder in children. It affects both boys and girls equally with prevalence estimates ranging from 5 to 10 percent to as high as 17.5 percent. Reading disability exists on a continuum, with dyslexia representing the lower range of a normal distribution of reading ability.

Other learning disabilities reflect difficulties in focusing attention or processing visual and spatial information (also called nonverbal learning disability) or problems understanding social and emotional information.

**A specific language based disorder:** Although it was originally called "word blindness," dyslexia is *not* a disorder of the visual system where words or individual letters are seen backward. It is a language disorder. Children sometimes say they have problems "seeing" the words, but this is a metaphorical description. There is little evidence of a significant correlation between early visuo-spatial or visuo-motor problems and later reading ability. Poor readers are as adept as good readers at copying visually confusable letters and words from memory, but they are significantly less good at naming or pronouncing these items on second exposure. Thus, the poor naming of letter or word forms is due to less well-established verbal codes rather than to visual-perceptual deficits.

Programs for dyslexia that offer visual-perceptual training have generally been found ineffective in improving the reading of dyslexics, as have those that focus on diet or medication for vestibular dysfunction.

**Of constitutional origin:** In other words, you are born with it. In a recent study, auditory evoked potentials (a measure of synchronous brain cell activity in response to a stimuli) to speech and nonspeech syllables discriminated between newborns that eight years later would be characterized as poor, dyslexic, or normal readers. Infants at risk for developmental dyslexia had a lot of difficulty resolving rapidly changing sounds (which are one hallmark of the special sounds that make up language) of any sort.

*Constitutional* refers to the fact that the reading problem was not due to the results of a head injury or an illness such as severe recurrent ear infections (which might affect the ability to hear and discriminate sounds) or any other acute source. The term *constitutional* also refers to the fact that dyslexia has a strong familial component. Forty percent of dyslexic children also have an affected sibling, and studies have reported anywhere from 23 percent to 65 percent of children who have a dyslexic parent also have dyslexia.

Finally, the term *constitutional* means that dyslexia will not go away. A dyslexic child can be taught to read, but dyslexia is a chronic and lifelong processing difficulty. A follow-up study of a group of children diagnosed with persistent reading failure in grades two through six, found that even after these children learned to read, they still read slower than other children. They continued to show problems with phonological awareness and word finding as adolescents. Reading remains effortful, even for the brightest dyslexic children. In the past, it was felt that the best possible outcome would be that dyslexic children could be taught compensatory reading strategies so their lives weren't defined by dyslexia. However, recent research from several labs using functional magnetic resonance imaging to study the results of remediation programs that increase phonological awareness suggests that after training, dyslexic children start to use the same parts of their brain to read as their normally reading peers.

The one good thing about the constitutional nature of dyslexia is that the underlying processes that go awry can be picked up very early by specific disparities in the child's development. These are all the signs I ignored with David. For example, David could never remember anyone's name or say which relative was an aunt, a cousin, or a grandfather. His large vocabulary often covered the fact that he couldn't retrieve the more common word, asking at age four to "Go to the emporium," because he couldn't recall the word *store*. He insisted on his green shirt when he wanted a blue one and was adamant about getting a roast beef sandwich, only to be disappointed when it wasn't turkey. He still calls his beloved grandmother "Dorsi," having inverted Doris, because the order of the sounds in the word isn't stable for him. He could build amazing things with Legos and pattern blocks, but he couldn't tell you which shape was a square and which was a circle. He could *not* learn the letters. Somewhere, I knew something was wrong, but I wasn't yet ready to find out what, to give it a name. This was a mistake, because the earlier you get your child help, the better off they will be. Ages four through seven are ideal.

**Characterized by difficulties in single word decoding:** *Decoding* is a fancy word for the ability to translate written symbols into recognizable words. The reading process can be broken into two elements: decoding and comprehension, or understanding. In dyslexia, higher-order cognitive abilities such as comprehension, vocabulary, and the ability to understand syntax remain intact. A dyslexic reader, because he has trouble hearing and sequencing the sounds that make up words, will have difficulty translating the written symbols into sounds, blending them together, then identifying that combination of sounds with a known word. He might try to guess the word from its first letter, reading *hat* for *had* or *sheep* for *sleep*. It is usually easiest for dyslexic children to hear the beginning consonants in words, rather than those at the end or middle. Vowel sounds, particularly in English, are hard because a vowel makes a different sound depending on what other letters are in the word. For example, an "e" on the end of a word makes the vowel in the middle of the word say its name, or long sound, like the "e" on the word *lame* changes the sound from "lam" where the "a" makes a soft sound. Often a reading guess is made on the basis of the shape of the word. For example, *sheep* and *sleep* have a similar visual configuration. What truly identifies a dyslexic child is the inability to read nonsense words, like *zirdn't,* which might be read as "dirty," when the child recognizes the d, i, r, and t and tries to put them into a word he knows, ignoring the sequence of the sounds.

Although dyslexic children usually have adequate listening comprehension skills, their difficulty decoding gets in the way of their understanding printed material. For example, if you decode the word *shore* as *horse*, it's going to be hard to get to the beach.

**Usually reflecting insufficient phonological processing abilities:** A phoneme is the smallest identifiable segment of speech. Phonological processing is the ability to become aware that speech can be broken down into phonemes (sounds) and that these phonemes are represented by printed forms. When we speak (unlike with written words), we don't speak in separate phonemes. Instead, the sounds are overlapped with one another so we can speak at a reasonable pace. This is what makes speech easy, but makes it hard for some children to break down the word into its component sounds and match them up with print. For example, the word *bat* is actually three phonemes (b / a / t /), but it seems like one sound. When you learn to read, you can recognize *bat* only if you can segment the word into its underlying phonological elements. You have to know that *bat* has three phonemes and is, therefore, represented by three letters. For most of us, this goes on automatically and unconsciously, but not for dyslexic readers. They have to be specifically taught to hear and attend to the phonological structure of speech, either through using alternate sensory channels to reinforce the sound-letter combination, or through using the motor image of the speech sound (the feeling a sound makes on the lips and tongue) to reinforce the association.

A second independent factor that contributes to dyslexia is known as rapid automatized naming or RAN. It is the ability to rapidly retrieve a label for an object that one already knows, like the name of a familiar person or a color. Reading involves being able to quickly match an abstract written symbol with a sound. Problems with rapid automatized naming will, therefore, affect reading speed.

Dyslexia reflects specific alterations in brain function that result in phonological processing problems that lead to measurable failures on school based tasks. Functional brain imaging studies electrophysiology, and postmortem brain specimens all suggest differences in the left temporo-parietal-occipital brain regions between dyslexic and nonimpaired readers. Recent research focuses on the angular gyrus, an area in the back of the brain that sits at the junction of the temporal, occipital, and parietal lobe. Normally, the angular gyrus acts as a pathway in processing and integrating the sight and sound information that enables people to understand written language. There is a complex two-way communication between the left angular gyrus and the other areas that are utilized to process visual and auditory information. The aberrant brain mechanisms for reading are present in dyslexic children who are just starting to read, so they cannot be blamed on the effects of a lifetime of poor reading. Imaging studies suggest that even after they have learned to read, dyslexic readers do not make any of the functional connections in the left angular gyrus that normal readers make.

Brain imaging studies support the notion of identical brain processes in all dyslexics. Dyslexia is dyslexia in any language. However, the writing systems of some languages are more complicated than others. English has 1,120 ways of spelling its 40 phonemes. Italian, in contrast, has what's called a transparent or shallow orthography, where the letters of the alphabet are in most instances uniquely mapped to each of the speech sounds occurring in the language. Italians need only thirty-three combinations of letters to spell out twenty-five phonemes. So reading Italian takes a lot less effort and, as a result, there are almost no Italians identified as dyslexic by their educational system. An Italian dyslexic will continue to read more slowly, as will all dyslexic children who have become proficient readers through remediation. French, where the mapping between letters, speech sounds, and whole word sounds is often highly ambiguous, is not a good choice for your dyslexic child's foreign language requirement.

Short of moving to a villa in Tuscany, getting help with phonological processing still remains the best bet in the treatment of dyslexia.

**These difficulties in single word decoding are often unexpected in relation to age and other cognitive and academic abilities:** Part of the definition of dyslexia is that there is *at least* average intelligence. Dyslexic children are not stupid, even if they often feel that way. When you think about it, decoding, by itself, is pretty stupid. A is always A. Where's the imagination in that? There's no higher order cognition involved. You are either "wired" to read, or you have to be taught to do it consciously and with practice, reading becomes more automatic. But being able to decode print says nothing about your intellectual capabilities or your capacity to understand what you read.

**Dyslexia is manifested by variable difficulty with different forms of language, often including, in addition to reading problems, a conspicuous problem with acquiring proficiency in writing and spelling:** Reading is what we call a receptive language skill, like listening. You take in information. Writing and spelling are expressive language skills, kind of the print equivalent of talking. The same processes, which affect decoding, will also affect the ability to output the correct sequences of sounds in written work, and the same types of errors are often found in a dyslexic's reading and their spelling. It is not surprising that the same child who reads "sleep" as "sheep" will try to spell "look" as "lock," or "done" as "dun."


## Ten Signs Worth Paying Attention To

So that's what dyslexia means, but what is a parent to do? There are several early signs of processing difficulties that will affect reading. If a child has more than one or two of these, it is worthwhile to have a more complete evaluation done by a competent psychologist with a specialization in reading or a clinical neuropsychologist who can specify the processing difficulties as well as the channels through which the child is most likely to learn the letter-sound connection.

• Not being able to name letters or sing the alphabet song, particularly in the context of a good vocabulary.

• Having trouble identifying words that begin with the same sound from a printed list or being unable to tell if two one-syllable words sound the same or different (e.g., "get" and "bet" or "sit" and "sat"). Children starting kindergarten should be able to recognize beginning and ending sounds.

• Problems rhyming or recognizing rhymes.

• Problems with phonological awareness—being able to identify and sequence the sounds within words (e.g., "If I took the word *bat* and took out the *b*, what word would be left?").

• Not knowing color or shape names.

• Speech and articulation problems, particularly those that involve oromotor praxis.

• Trouble remembering automated sequences like numbers or days of the week.

• Problems with fine motor activities like drawing a circle or copying letters, or gross motor sequences like jumping jacks or riding a tricycle.

• Trouble retrieving specific words (e.g., naming a picture of a familiar object, a tendency to substitute a less frequently used similar meaning word for a target word, or the substitution of semantically related words such as apple for orange, truck for car).

• Sequencing errors in speech ("Dorsi" for "Doris").

• Trouble with verbal memory—difficulty recalling a sentence or story that was just told.

*Books, books, books books.* But not one had the answer for me! Anyway, I already knew most of the stuff I found. I could have written those books. Now the terms drift meaningless before my eyes. Which hemisphere is responsible for language? What are the cerebral asymmetries? The brain anomalies? Getting the information wasn't the problem. The problem was that it was *my son*. The problem was that I was too incapacitated to make use of anything the books told me. David seemed afraid of the letters. Where's the locus of fear in the brain? Not one book told me how frustrated I'd feel, how impotent and unable to save him.

**PART II**

It Doesn't Look Like Kansas Anymore:
Initial Reactions

# Chapter 4

# The Perfect Child

*Maybe it was the speech. Was he always afraid that no one could understand him? I understood him, mostly, but sometimes it was really a challenge. He had a sign language, twirling his fingers in the air to mean "airplane," whoosh meant "train," claps signaled "yes." He would say "lobfo" when he wanted the red stuffed animal lobster cousin Alex gave him. His favorite. He left it in a taxi and I called the taxi commission to get it back. Did I know something then, that I was so solicitous of his every wish? Was it just that he was my first, or did I already know something was wrong? Everyone saying "What? What?" to him must have made him feel defeated, like he couldn't get what he wanted or take care of himself. I learned to talk for him, maybe too much, finishing his sentences, making his bridge to the world. He couldn't make himself speak right, so he got quiet. Better that than people screwing up their faces quizzically, or other kids telling him to stop spitting when he couldn't control the saliva in his mouth. Why wasn't I bothered when he didn't speak by eighteen months? He still doesn't speak to many other people.*

*He was more passive than other kids; it was hard for him*

to do physical activities. Funny how being read to was his most intense pleasure. When his mouth muscles developed to the point where he could talk better, he had an amazing vocabulary. He understood all those books we read to him, but he just couldn't respond, he couldn't generate a lot of language. Why didn't I get him help with the speech earlier? Why did I listen to people who told me to wait, that he was just socially anxious?

He never could stand new situations unless I was with him. If I was there, he could be fearless. He hated birthday parties because he didn't know what to do at them. New kids, new faces whose names he couldn't remember, no routine he could have memorized. When he was eighteen months, he got afraid of clowns. Found every clown in the world, in the corners of children's books, at the merry-go-round in Central Park, on a balloon. We rented a cottage that summer from some artist who made shrunken heads out of old coconuts. "Oh no, Larry, look!" I said, hysterical "Clowns." Who could ever imagine so many clowns? Did anyone ever notice how scary and angry clowns are?

The other fear was the Peruvian child. The Peruvian child. Right after Dan was born, David saw a picture of a mummy of a Peruvian child who had been preserved by being dried out. David was so angry then. He thought the child was being punished. He got afraid of being dried out himself and started drinking all the time, trying to hold in his pee. Nearly drove us crazy trying to figure out what he was talking about. Throwing himself on the ground, moaning "I'm the Peruvian child." "No you are not," I told him. "You are from the Upper West Side of Manhattan." What mother would know what to do? He always had a mind that ran ahead of his ability to understand, terrible tantrums, and a ferocious temper in the twos. Sometimes we would just have to say "Oh well, at least it didn't last as long as yesterday's."

Oh God, what will happen to him?

None of these things—his fears, his speech, his poor sleep—
bothered me then. David was perfect to me. Perfect. The funniest child.
I loved his obvious, serious intellect. When, at two, David became
interested in trucks, a mother who had previously called anything bigger than a Chevy an "earth mover" could now identify the cherry
picker, the forklift, and the Bobcat frontloader. And it was no false
passion. I wanted to know what David wanted to know. I would see
him in his room with a Richard Scarry book "studying," mouthing the
names of the trucks as he pointed to their pictures. Looking back, his
obsessive need to collect information was disturbing, but at the time
it charmed me. Every day was a smile. This was the child I was meant
to have.

## Mourning

After years of having minuscule galley kitchens that left the wish to
drink a cup of coffee sitting down a daily unsatisfied desire, I now own
the kitchen of my dreams—a h-u-g-e refrigerator, a stove with a grill,
cabinets with room for double packages of cereals, 48 oz. ketchups,
15 rolls of paper towels. It is a kitchen designed for a perpetually
beautiful mother. Pirouetting to pop the tuna casserole into the oven,
her hair unwinds (only slightly) from her French knot. Her handsome
husband rushes home to mow the lawn. It is a kitchen catering to
armies of unruly, happy children, running in from school, throwing
their backpacks full of homework on the large oak table.

My triumphant fantasies evaporate with David's diagnosis. My
kitchen becomes a private prison. Feral squirrels chase each other as I
stare absently out the window at days that feel gray despite their bright
color. My face reflects in the glass. Old . . . older. I'll never be that
beautiful woman now. I wake early, believing for more than a moment
that I'm back in my single bed in Queens, listening to kids shrieking
excitedly on the playground six floors below. I can't join them. Memories of long buried humiliations mix with my worries—the day in
third grade I forgot to put on a skirt, a tough girl named Lisa saying

I was too uncool to have her name, a slam book entry: "Beautiful hair but nothing else."

I imagine neurons migrating mysteriously in fetal brains, moving to new places, forming odd connections, losing others. At the periphery of my fear: David, working at some menial job, where people like me are rude to him.

I misplace everything, losing one of the diamonds from my mother's wedding ring; walking up Madison Avenue, desperately re-tracing my steps, I try to find the place where everything was still in my possession. Sweaters put in the washing machine come back doll-size. Books disappear. Credit cards and licenses fall over the event horizon, sucked into a black hole. Sometimes the items mysteriously reappear, in just the place I've looked earlier. Each mishap feels critical. If I can't have that particular thing back, I will die.

Surely, I could have prevented this. Like a well-worn litany, I re-view the roster of my sins. Over and over. And again. Maybe it was the chain letter I didn't answer when I was pregnant with Dan. Was it too late to send it on now, two years later?

I am assaulted by the written word. Everywhere words demand to be read—signs, directions on the oatmeal box, price tags on clothing.

### FAB DEEP CLEANS! SMELLS GREAT!

### EXIT 17
#### Dobbs Ferry/Ardsley

TURN OFF MICROWAVE BEFORE OPENING.

### *Diet* COKE

Rotating the newspaper upside down, I feel for what words look like to David. Even when the letters are recognizable, like "o," the order is mixed up. The brain is wired to recognize patterns, to seek understanding, to find structures that make the world predictable. What's the minimum information for recognizing the letter "b"? When does the pattern become automatic, nonrandom, no longer necessitat-ing conscious thought? A straight line alone could be an "l" or a "d" or an "h." Add a curve. Depending on the way it faces, could be a "d" or, where it's placed, a "p." David is right. The letters are meaningless squiggles. They are senseless, repulsive, impossible. I pretend to myself that they are something other than letters. Lovely "b," now a pregnant woman, "C" my morning touch-my-toes sit-up. If I can "catch" dyslexia, maybe I can take it away from David. When he was sick as an infant, I would kiss him, hoping the illness would pass into my stronger body.

My self-indulgence knows no bounds. David has a reading problem. Other parents contend with far worse. Despair is my special bond with David, our fates entwined in a knot that is my deepest pleasure and the source of my most egregious errors. Who wants to read anyway?

# Chapter 5

# Lissa Weinstein, Ph.D.

"Hoping to cheer up a few patients, Lissa?" Larry asks in his usual beguiling manner, as I prepare to face the office dressed in black for the fifth day in a row. Why not wear black? Black is the truth.

I've always loved the pacing of a day broken into fifty-minute hours. My office is a sparsely set stage, its lack of clues to my identity allowing room for my patients' dramas to materialize. The blinds drawn for privacy, the rug worn from the endless rubbing of nervous feet, the arms of the deep leather chairs bare from inadvertent scratching, and shelves and shelves of books. With adults, I sit in the pine rocker my mother picked up for $25 at a garage sale, waiting for the temptations of the everyday to fade, allowing the lost continents of childhood to emerge.

Children can't tell you their problems; they let you know through their play. Seven-year-old tough-girl Edie* studies me suspiciously in the waiting room, hiding the grimy face she does not yet know is beautiful under a Yankee cap. Her slit eyes allow little light into an already dim world. Since her father died the prior spring from lupus, she has been stabbing at her two-year-old sister with forks and pencils. Edie believes she has come to therapy as punishment for her bad behavior.

*For the purpose of confidentiality the patient vignettes are composites.

"Dr. Lissa Weinstein doesn't understand children," Edie hollers, making sure my colleagues in the next office can hear. "She is very mean to them. Don't send her any more patients." It's not our worst day. Sometimes, she gets into my office first and locks me out, forcing me to beg for entry. Edie is no stranger to humiliation.

When she first came to see me, Edie tried hard to be a good girl, insisting we have "fun" and listen to music. She wanted me to bring her things from my home. They were *never* right—the construction paper was the wrong color, the stapler was too small. I tried to get her better things, failing to grasp what she couldn't yet put into words. She is missing . . . something, something that can never be replaced or fixed, not only her father, who she never mentions, but a way she wants to feel about herself. Now, every session brings forth more rage. It is unbearable to be in the room with her.

Edie, starting a craft project, pours Elmer's glue over her hands, transfixed by its milky stickiness. Desperate for a way to make contact with her, I ask, "Would you like to pour it on my hands, too, so I can know what it feels like?"

Thrilled, Edie dumps glue out over my hands, watching it snake down my arms. "Sit still. Don't move!" she shrieks, high on the power of her suddenly released rage. Grabbing my upper arms so hard that her thumbs leave deep indentations, she tries to glue globs of Play-Doh on me. "How do you feel now, Miss Doctor Lissa?"

Deep in the jungle of my unconscious reveries, I meet Edie, temporarily residing. Following a hunch, I talk as her. Words pour out of my mouth, oddly unstoppable. "It's horrible. Look at me. Look at these things on my body. Everyone will know that there is something wrong with me. I can never go out. I can't be with the other kids now. I'm different. Everyone can see."

"Yes, *you* are disgusting, Lissa. No one would want you around. And do you ever think it can be better?"

"I will always feel this ugly?"

"Yes, yes, you will. And you will be more ugly. More ugly than you can imagine. You want to die from being so ugly. Everyone hates you. You are going to the camp. The camp for crazy children."

Her self-hatred is excruciating to grasp. Edie, however, is exultant. For a moment she has made me feel what she feels; she is no longer alone, a girl made repulsive by loss and rage. I have lent her language, our first step in articulating the story that will allow her to feel whole again. But the journey into her world opened a portal into my own shame since David's diagnosis, reaching down into my own fear of imperfection.

I glance at the letter telling me that I have won an award for some papers I have written. *Papers no one in their right mind would ever read.* They are difficult papers, concerning the work of Lev Vygotsky, a Russian semiotician who started an Instututute of Defectology in Moscow in the 1930s as part of a program to educate the backward peasants.

I lie down on the analytic couch, exhausted after a poor night. The memory of last night's dream returns. I am wandering through the surreal landscape of *One Fish Two Fish Red Fish Blue Fish*, a Dr. Seuss beginner book I have been trying—unsuccessfully—to get David to read with me.

The dream scene is a mixture of two pages. There is a street sign, with directional arrows, one pointing "To THERE," another pointing "To HERE." The words on the actual page in the book read:

> From there to here,
> from here to there,
> funny things are everywhere.

Odd and unnatural animals from another page are walking in an endless line across the uneven, hilly terrain. Not one looks normal. Although they do not appear in the dream, the words on the other page are remembered upon my awakening:

> Some have two feet
> and some have four.
> Some have six feet
> And some have more.
> Where do they come from?

I can't say.

But I bet they have come a long, long way.

In the dream I am lost. I stare at the sign, unable to read it. It is immediately clear, with the certainty unique to dreams, that I have not won the coveted award. How could I win? I can't read, much less write. Maybe I am one of the freakish six-footed creatures, but no, I'm only an observer. I tell myself that I'm not the strange one, but of course I believe I am.

How does one get from here to there? From not reading to reading. From not knowing to knowing. From not belonging to having a place. The dream is agony, like the dreams I had after getting my doctorate, finding myself back in high school, realizing that I hadn't done any of the reading for my human biology course and the exam is today.

How can I do what David cannot, how can I have what he cannot? I'm nowhere in the world, too, all separate from the spaces that once nurtured me. I stop writing papers. I have nothing to say.

The buzzer sounds for my next patient, interrupting my reverie. Pulled back to the tyranny of the present tense, I quickly dry the tears that erupt without warning. The doctor *is* in. I find comfort in the anonymity of work, the necessary distance providing a welcome shield.

Checking my appointment book—11:00: Mrs. Trant. It's not a meeting I'm looking forward to. Several weeks earlier she had consulted me about her adolescent daughter, whom she believed had an undiagnosed learning disability.

"Well, Maria has always been an excellent student, usually As and high Bs. But this year she's been struggling. I've always felt there was something wrong."

"Has the school suggested testing?" I ask.

"Well, not exactly. I felt she might need untimed testing. She'll be taking the SAT tests this year, and I really want her to do her best."

"Has there been any history of school problems? Did she have any trouble learning to read? Any difficulty paying attention?"

"Well, no."

It doesn't sound right, but I've learned that sometimes mothers see things that the school has missed. I agree to do the evaluation.

I've always enjoyed psychological testing, with its quick cross-section of a child's mind. Since David's diagnosis, testing is torture. I find myself comparing each child's abilities to David. Behind every question, I'm secretly thinking *Could David do this one?* Can he read the word *go,* recognize the letter "a"? But this evaluation is torture for another reason. Ten hours of testing later, it's clear the school is right. Mrs. Trant's daughter is a child of high average intelligence who has gotten by in her top private school through extensive tutoring. There are no signs of a specific reading disability or an attentional disorder. There is no reason to support extended time on her College Boards. She is *not* learning disabled.

Straight from the ladies who lunch at Sarabeth's, Mrs. Trant arrives clad in head-to-toe Armani, sporting Bulgari coin earrings and a strand-by-strand highlighting job that cost more than my car. I report the findings of the extensive test battery.

"Well, I'd like you to suggest that she needs extra time on tests," she says.

"There's no evidence to support that conclusion," I reply, steeling myself for the confrontation.

"Well, without good test scores, she won't be able to apply to the best schools."

"So you want to have the best chance to up her scores, because she'll do better if she has more time?" I ask, already starting to cross over the line from professional neutrality into accusation. *My son is dyslexic. He will never read as quickly as other children. He needs the extra time so his deficits don't hide his abilities.* "I'm sorry. I can't write that in the report. It wouldn't be honest."

Mrs. Trant is not insulted. She feels that using her money to get the very best chance for her daughter is acceptable. Why shouldn't her daughter go to Harvard? But I am livid, straining my limited reserves of professional demeanor to not scream at her.

Mrs. Trant's lips purse, her nostrils flare slightly, and there is an almost imperceptible tightening in her neck tendons before her all-purpose graciousness prevails. "Very well then. You'll send me a bill, of course." She offers her hand.

**PART III**

Follow the Yellow Brick Road:
We Start to Get Help

# Chapter 6

# Kindergarten

Ms. Miller looks nervous but welcoming. After having seen copies of the speech evaluation, the occupational therapy evaluation, and the "full neuropsychological," she has called me in to talk about strategies for the classroom.

I've donned my best parental clothing for this long march back to room 103. I'm trying to follow the advice I always give other parents—be straightforward with the school. Otherwise, they treat your child as if he is slow or lazy or poorly behaved rather than learning disabled.

"Is it all right if Mrs. Wilson comes, too?"

"Sure," I say, still feeling awkward that I refused to let Mrs. Wilson do the speech evaluation.

Ms. Miller continues, "I've never seen such complete reports. Very helpful. Especially the speech evaluation. You know, I had speech problems as a child. I was in an accident and I felt very bad for a long time, but I worked and overcame them. You'd be surprised what children can do." *Now I understand the tears on Open School Night.* "David has been somewhat of a puzzle to me, because he's very sweet, but he can't focus on learning letters. I thought maybe he had attention deficit disorder."

"Not at all," I concur. "Actually, he has the most focused attention

I've ever seen. It's his strong suit. It's really much more a language problem for him. The attention is just . . . Well, how long could you pay attention if people were speaking Greek to you? That's what the letters are like for him. They have no meaning. Look. Every other kid colors the whole letter one color. Look at David's 'S.' It's red polka dots on the top, brown stripes on the bottom. It's just a design, not a letter that represents a sound written down. Looking at the letters makes him feel terrible. He'd do anything to avoid them—that's why his behavior looks like attention problems."

Ms. Miller asks, "What do you think we can do to improve his reading in the classroom? I'm getting a Masters in reading from Teachers College. I try to bring in a lot of remediation techniques to my kindergartners."

Ms. Miller is a beauty. She's speaking in such a rush that she is nearly breathless. She's so excited, eager to share what she's learned.

She continues, "Like on Name Day, I sneak in a phonics lesson using the first letter of their name, getting them to rhyme and find other words that start with that letter and using the letter in a song. We make letter drawings using pasta shapes and try to form the letters with our bodies. It's all reinforcing the basic knowledge through different sensory modalities. What do you think, Mrs. Wilson?"

"Well, I was looking at the speech evaluation, and David has trouble retrieving words, so I think he shouldn't be called on in class unless he raises his hand, in order to spare him any possible embarrassment."

"Wow, that's incredible," I say impressed and grateful for this simple suggestion. *How could I not have trusted her?* "What other remedial help can the school give him?"

Ms. Miller looks embarrassed. "Well, nothing right now. The school doesn't expect children to be reading in kindergarten, so there's no program for him."

"But we know he's not going to read. He has all the underlying processing problems that predict to dyslexia. Everyone knows intervention between the ages of five and seven is most effective. Talk about catch-22." I'm flabbergasted.

"We're sorry. We can't offer preventive medicine. A child has to be behind grade level to get services."

*Could this really mean that I have had my son diagnosed only to*

*find out that there is nothing to be done? Except now I see*
*ferently, in a way that can only make him feel worse? Great.*

Ms. Miller looks away. She knows I'm right. Like so many, she is a good teacher caught in a system trying to save money.

Another part of me is happy there's no treatment. Maybe I still want to pretend it will go away. Maybe because now I can hide at home with him. In a moment's epiphany, I realize I must teach David to read myself. I will make everything okay again.


## The Sword in the Stone

So hi ho, hi ho, it's off to work we go. Calling on all my fairyland heroes for help, I'm the Seven Dwarfs saving Snow White, Merlin coaching King Arthur to pull his shoulders back like a falcon in order to grab that sword from the stone, Peter Pan teaching Wendy to crow, and Cinderella's fairy godmother. On a good day.

On a bad day, I'm completely unable to simply take pleasure in what David has to tell me or what he wants to learn about. Every activity is screened—how will this help him read, to retrieve information? I can't simply be with him. I'm always trying to move him somewhere.

"Here David, why don't you try this computer program? It'll be fun. It's about counting." No response. He looks sullen at my offer of *How Many Bugs in a Box.*

"I'm not a books kind of guy. I'm just a toy guy. I was made to buy a lot of toys. Do you think I could have a new Beast Wars toy? Do you? Daddy says I can. All right? Okay?"

"What could you possibly want?" I ask, unable to disguise my exasperation. "You never play with these things for more than a day."

"I don't know, I really don't know. How should I know?" David sags deeper into the couch.

Dan comes in and makes some slapstick face to make me laugh.

"You always laugh with Dan and not with me,"

This is what he observes. This is what he can say. David is five, and he has only five-year-old words. Each word is a world of worry; they are so condensed, his thoughts not yet connecting with his language. Everything is crammed into stupid phrases like "Sorry" or "Dinner wasn't good tonight." We look at each other across a wide chasm, unable to articulate what we long for; no words. What can we say to each other without making things worse? Only the wrong words, words we hang onto like a lifeline that still won't save us.

I know what he wants. He wants me to look at him with the gleam that should be in a mother's eye. "Du bist shoen Maidele" my grandmother would say, a "pretty girl," seeing me and helping me see myself as perfect. Isn't that a child's birthright, to never have to ward off the questioning glance, the disgusted look when he is unable to do something, or refuses to try, or sits listlessly hours and hours in front of the TV, unable to know his own pain? He wants me to have fun with him, like we used to before all this happened, when he was just my wonderful, clearly original child. I cannot hide my disappointment.

We have become used to the silence.

A sleepwalker, my body shifts into a familiar stance from an old photograph of my mother. Arms crossed, her red nails dig tensely into the flesh above her elbows. Her eyes blaze blind, blind with defiant anger. She is closed to me, and now I am her, closed to David.

*It is a very hot, sticky summer in the 1950s. It is the height of the polio scare. Mommy is buying me shoes. I have flat feet and Mommy feels that I must wear "cookies" in my Buster Brown shoes to force the arch. I have to walk on a high platform in front of a shoe "expert." Will he tell me that I need braces? That I won't walk again, like the children I have heard the parents whisper sadly about? "Poor things" they say. Mommy is fierce in her insistence that I can improve, that I will have the feet of a dancer. She will check my wet footprints on the mat as I step out naked after the bath to see if the "treatment" is working.*

I'm the evil stepmother, Morgan le Fay, the witch offering Snow White the poison apple. There are no real gifts from me anymore. I approach his reading like a military campaign—full frontal attack. I make pillows in different textures for each letter so David can feel them as well as name them. I create theater with the Letter People. I make sand letter paintings and pretzel letters. I print large tags to put around his room—WALL, CLOSET, LAMP, DESK. I *am* helping. *I am helping*. When my hypomanic efforts seem to work, I am ecstatic. My sense of personal triumph suggests I am trying to fix some problem of mine through him.

Over and over I try to force him, and he is still such a little boy and has no way into the words and letters and can't figure out how to do what I want from him or even what I want. It makes him sad and mad. He needs something, he needed something from me, maybe it was this toy, maybe it was the first pancake, no he didn't really like that pancake anyway, no not the second pancake—that's burnt from the butter, could I make him waffles, no those waffles have too big holes and there's too much syrup, you always put on too much syrup.

David stares away from me as I try to get him to name the letters in William Steig's name on the cover of his book. He turns suddenly, spitting the words.

"You made this happen to me. You made me look at the letters when I wasn't ready. You made me hate them. You made me feel stupid." The veins are popping on his forehead. He's held this in a long time. His bitterness a rodent, running so rapidly across the room that a moment later we tell ourselves we've never seen it.

There is a price to pay for my success in teaching him the letters. I can't see the world with him anymore. Now I sit opposite, a detective ferreting out clues of his imperfection. Judging, watching, evaluating. David, with his sixth sense for my anxiety, sees my nervous look when he can't name a letter, hears my silence when another mother brags her child is reading already, and feels my impatience when I tie his shoes. He looks at himself with my disenchanted eyes, my fear of the unknown.

I'm the expert. I should know what to do. But I'm as lost as any other parent. Should I get a tutor? Officially classify him as learning disabled? Send him to a school designed specifically for the teaching of reading? And worst of all, as first grade rolls in, how much do I need to tell him? How much does he already know?

## The Letter People

I knew that it would be hard to read by the end or maybe the middle of kindergarten. I had friends in my nursery school who knew all their letters, but it didn't make any difference to me then. I still couldn't recognize my name in kindergarten, but I had a very nice teacher who would always read my card last or next to last so it was easy to pick out. There was another David in my class, but his last name started with M, so on the cards they would call us David S, and David M. The other kids just had their first name, so all I really had to look for was the S after the D.

At first the letters didn't make any sense to me at all. I couldn't even recognize them. They just looked like squiggles of nothing. In kindergarten they wanted us to learn to write our names. I did it like it was a painting that I was copying. At first I'd just write DVD. In school we would have to write our names and then glue pasta over the letters and say the letters as we ran our fingers over the pasta. I didn't like doing that.

Then I started to recognize the letters. I would copy them over and over. I would pick a letter and try to find it in a bunch of writing. I had a hard time learning the names of the letters. I would call them other things, things I could remember, like E was called three flags or F was two flags, A was the Eiffel tower, or L was for Larry and Lissa. Sometimes I couldn't remember their names at all. Mommy would look kind of something when I couldn't name them, like sad? I didn't know, but then I wanted to stop looking at them. Who named those letters anyway? I knew in some other countries they had different alphabets and that the letters were called other things. Mommy told me that when we went to the museum and I asked about the different writings.

There was something that helped me in kindergarten. My teacher had these things called the Letter People. I liked them so much I got Mommy to order my own. Each letter was a person and it did something. Then the letters weren't just squiggles anymore. To me they were like real people, like stories, like friends. The vowels were girls. The boys were consonants. Miss A. was sneezing. She said "Ah Choo"; Mr. D was eating "delicious donuts." My favorite was Mr. S. He would put on his Super Socks, which "suddenly" changed him into a "supersonic streak in the sky." They had great music. Y could be a girl or a boy. I guess you could say he was "gay," but I didn't know what that was when I was in kindergarten. Now I see that each letter made its sound, but then it just helped me remember the letter names. There was a tape with songs of the Letter People which we would dance to at school. Mommy found the Letter People in Boston. We got the tape and the Letter People puppets. We blew up the puppets and made up stories with them. We made plays. We married Q and U. That way I could remember they always went together. I would still get mixed up about which things were letters and which were numbers, so we made up a play about O who used to think he was nothing (a zero). The puppets sang "You're not really nothing. You are special. You are a vowel." I used to carry the songs of the Letter People with me everywhere with my tape recorder. It drove my parents crazy when we'd have to go in the car to Boston and I'd play the Letter People all the way. Over and over. I loved the Letter People. I thought about them all the time. After a while, it seemed like all at once, I did learn the letter sounds and letter names. Sometimes I would make up my own letter people. Like Mr. X. He was all mixed up in his body, but not in his mind. We had Letter People videos, too. They tried to tell you how to put the sounds together. But I didn't like those. I only liked the Letter People themselves.

I grew out of the Letter People. Now I think they are stupid. When Dan plays the tape, I make fun of them. Whatever happened to the Letter People? Oh yeah, Dan put holes in them. He took them hostage.

We did lots of other things with the letters, too. We made letters out of Legos. We made letter pretzels with salt so that I could feel the letters as well as look at them. We made letter cookies. We tried to find the letters in other shapes. We made letter shapes with our bodies. People kept telling me the letters over and over again. It was hard to remember them at first. I memorized them. Everyone talked about the letters in kindergarten, and I talked about it a lot. After a while, I could name the letters but I couldn't read and I could see there were people who could read. All the other kids.

## Other Approaches

Walking up the hill, David holds his purple My First Sony tape recorder in one hand and Larry's hand in the other. Larry's large protective hands envelop David's weaker grasp with his own firm one. Larry keeps exactly to David's dawdling pace—not an easy task for Larry, who is really a walk-fast kind of guy. *Songs of the Letter People* blare from the tape recorder. We are up to Mr. D., who is singing about his donuts, delicious donuts: Ms. E. will soon be exercising. The vowel sounds are always women, and they are angry about having to work so much harder than the male consonants. One by one the Letter People contribute their sounds. Mr. K. tells you that you can "Kick a ball and you can kick a can, but you can never ever kick a man." That's a message we need to hear in our house—never kick a living younger brother. Mr. X. is all mixed up, but just in his body, David has told me, not in his mind.

A warm afternoon in late April. Prisms of bright color emanate from bulbs miraculously spared by deer; purple flowers of Vinca minor spike up from their deep evergreen leaves. Larry and David walk through three whole renditions of the twenty-six songs of the Letter People, one for each letter of the alphabet. They walk and walk, not really needing words at all.

## Birthday Card

> *Dear David,*
>     *Here are some books on dinosaurs and the human body for your mother to read to you. They would be too hard for any kid to read.*
>     *Love, Aunt Hillary*

## Mary, Mary Quite Contrary: How Does Your Garden Grow?

Even before the snow lifts, the gardening catalogues arrive. In the suburbs, as soon as you have an address you're magically connected to some ubiquitous catalogue universe. I've never grown anything more complicated than houseplants, which miraculously survived in an apartment with no natural light until they were decapitated by the venetian blinds.

But now, Wayside Gardens, the Complete Clematis, Breck's Bulbs, and Carlson's Gardens are taking a predatory interest in my salvation. Tempting pictures of lush, overgrown plants, hideously fertile and psychedelic, bid me welcome. Seas of bulbs that would "naturalize" into a vision of Holland. Deerproof.

I always react to loss with a need to improve my surroundings. My sadness over David makes me want to fix things, to make things grow. No . . . to force them to grow if that's what it takes. I want a garden. A *successful* garden.

But not all those obscenely cheerful plants. No cotton-candy dahlias, salmon impatiens, fire-orange marigolds. Never! My tastes run toward the subtle and salacious joys of the shade garden. A garden without color, natural but sparse, truthful in a barren sort of way. Ferns, hostas, dark leafy plants that will gratefully grow, no matter what I offer.

Both the terrain and my talents are poorly suited to this frenzied passion. The backyard is rock and scrub, with soil only thick enough to hide the broken beer bottles of the hobos and rebellious teenagers who claimed the forest before us. Where others see a barren, sunless quarter-acre, my needy imagination creates a stunning natural garden. I start composting. There's a vegetable patch in the future. Should the incipient nuclear attack of my Cold War girlhood materialize, I will be prepared! I can grow my own food; I can survive all disasters. Can I dig a well?

I'm up with the dawn, ready to start searching out spots for possible plantings. I grab the thorny weeds with my bare hands, pulling muscles in my back while lifting the boulders that are the only things that grow here. I need to feel the soil, to smell its woodsy rejuvenation mysteriously developing from rotting, dank leaves.

Because of the thriving tick population, I wear long pants, socks tucked in, and spray myself head to toe with repellent. No Smith & Hawkins garden clogs, lovely loose-fitting dresses, or straw hats for keeping my flowing hair out of the sun for me. No wicker baskets to collect the vegetables for tonight's dinner. To the untrained eye, I was a poorly dressed, middle-age woman trying desperately to make something change. Now! Gloves? Those are for weekend gardeners.

David leaves the gate open to welcome the deer. Dan pipes up that the weeds are the most beautiful part of the garden because they make it look like "a real jungle." All spring, I hear their voices begging for attention, for food. "Can we have breakfast Mommy?" I hear them, but I can't respond. I'm weeding, making way for new beauty, digging a pathway to meaning.

The gardening book collection is vying for space on the shelves next to *The Standard Edition of the Complete Works of Sigmund Freud: Perennials, Gardening Techniques, Landscaping Nature, Plants and Flowers, Ferns, The Shade Garden, The Organic Gardener.* My nails are encrusted with dirt that I don't even bother to wash off before running to see patients; my hands are rough from handling the soil. I have no shame, not about my garden, anyway. I need something growing that I can control.

## Conversations We Don't Have

What really separates the city from suburbia is darkness . . . and silence. The sounds of nighttime traffic on Columbus Avenue, a forgetful mother running to get milk at the all-night bodega, and the ever-present salsa music wafting up from the street below are all gone. Here there is only quiet; no streetlamps serve us as distant beacons.

Larry and I lie in bed with space for another person between us. The stale, comforting smells of marriage, its ease—gone. Larry, still a handsome man, is warmed by his moth-eaten childhood sweater. I wrap myself in a single-size down quilt—a mommy's sarcophagus.

We inherited the Swedish modern furniture from my parents. I imagine their life on this bed. It could not have been this.

Pictures on the dresser offer no clues as to what is wrong. Larry, living in Berkeley in the sixties mischievously daring the camera, side by side photos of me and Dan as infants look surprisingly alike—Dave, curly haired at two with his Snoopy sip bottle, me at seven awkwardly smiling in my new blue plastic glasses—Pauline had cut my bangs herself. Our wedding picture. One clue. The children's school pictures propped in their "School Days" paper frames, impermanent.

"Lar?" I reach across the canyon, asking the same questions over and over. "Larry, do you think if we had gone to the hospital earlier . . . ?"

"Lissa, I'm trying to sleep. I have to be up early tomorrow."

What hides in silence? A laundry list of accusations.

"You're a doctor. You should have made sure they sectioned me."

"You never take him to speech."

"You don't see the problems."

Larry has his complaints, too. "You're so angry, Lissa. Don't you think David feels it?" I hear Larry say, "Didn't your mother's brother have two children who were retarded?" The words are vivid, hallucinatory, and cutting. They are real. Larry is half-asleep now, mumbling his course of action to correct the problems.

"Don't worry, Lissa. We've figured it out. It's the DNA. It's in the shape of the molecule, in the proteins. Everything will be all right. I've got the answer. Trust me. You should write down what I say."

He is far more optimistic about the possibilities.

"Everyone learns to read. It's a finite skill."

*Why doesn't this destroy you? I'm up at 4 A.M. every morning, nauseous from the minute I awake, thinking another day is here and David won't read. I look in the mirror, and I am falling back into the shadows, retreating into the creases in my face. "Your face could freeze that way," Pauline would say when I frowned.*

*You put on a suit every morning and your world is the same. You design studies, look for the gene for schizophrenia, and teach residents. People call you Dr. Siever, and you don't wonder who that is. They respect you. You feel you deserve it.*

I know he suffers disappointments, but I can't see them.

*Powerful men. Brilliant men. Larry, a presidential scholar; his father a Harvard professor. Eloquent under pressure. Larry can't know what it's like for David—looking for the word he can't find, the one he knows he had but just slipped into the void, standing there going "hmm, um," hoping to fake it while another word comes to him. Larry always knows where to run to meet the soccer ball. How will David manage?*

Imagining Larry's refrain; I hear him say:

"Oh, Lissa. You love to prepare for the worst. You worried he couldn't hold his head up at one month. Dr. Max told you by the time he gets to college he'll have head control. David is a rocket scientist. He'll be fine."

*What can Larry know? He stays in the real world. Schedules, obligations, facts! Larry is his father, but David is me. He came from my body. Larry didn't feel the doughy emptiness where his solid moving form had been, the longing to have him back.*

Larry is tired of the endless, grinding wave of my despair. Who wouldn't be? We never talk. If no one gives sorrow words, it doesn't exist. All along, we sat at a table set by our imagination and read books in libraries whose windows opened onto perpetually warm rain streets. What we didn't already have would come. But now the table is wrong. The fork sits in place of the spoon, and the napkin is folded incorrectly. The library never existed, its mahogany shelves mere fiberboard. Children glue marriages together, moving couples smoothly through a loss of beauty, a fading brilliance. We have problems, but our kids, our children are doing *so* well. We're a team with a purpose. We're the top. We're the Coliseum. But when that fantasy falls . . .

Who is this stranger? Fragments of sentences drop in the darkness between us.

# Chapter 7

# First Grade

The members of the Committee on Special Education (CSE) sit in a U-shape phalanx, facing me, armed with opinions and policies. My arsenal contains only indecision and a destructive wish to believe nothing is wrong with David. The meeting, taking place only weeks into first grade, has been convened because of David's speech problems. Individually, I feel fondly toward the women who constitute the Committee—the District Head of Special Education, David's teacher, the reading and speech specialists, and the school psychologist. In a group, they metamorphose. The District Head of Special Education looks at me with her helmet of frosted hair and a smile that does not inspire trust; David's grandmotherly, "let the child develop at his own pace", teacher looms, menacing.

It is the CSE's mandate to offer the child the "least restrictive setting." They recommend that David be classified as having a physically handicapping condition on the basis of his speech. This is a different category than Learning Disabled, and a child is less able to receive comprehensive services for reading in this classification. David will get speech therapy in school and occupational therapy to help strengthen his hand muscles so he can write the letters better.

*Wait. That's not what's wrong. It's not the muscle strength that keeps him from writing. He can't do the fine motor sequencing for print writing. Oh well. At least they can teach him to tie his shoes.* The District Head, satisfied that she has discharged her responsibilities, says, "Well, I think that's a plan."

"I don't think he's going to be able to read," my voice is small and childlike. *Lissa, what is going on? You sit on these committees all the time. You're known for being fierce. People hire you to fight for their children. Why are you being such a wimp?*

The District Head turns to the reading specialist, who says, "Well, I was really worried about him at the kindergarten screening." *Nobody ever told me.* "However, now, even though I really never make predictions, I think he's right on the cusp of reading. He's certainly on grade level."

There is some truth to what she is saying. By the end of kindergarten David had done a thorough job of teaching himself the letter-sound relationships by using the Letter People. He can hear initial and ending consonants. He knows his letters and colors, he can recognize Dan's name and the names of a few of the kids in his class, he knows a few sight words, and he can tell a story in a sensible order. I am eager for the school to tell me he won't need help, hoping to avoid the stigma of having him classified as Learning Disabled. That's the truth.

*Lissa, there are serious processing issues. You know he won't read. Fight for him.* "Dr. Weinstein" might be a killer, able to be aggressive on a child's behalf, but Lissa Siever is paralyzed.

I leave the meeting knowing I've done the wrong thing, but also happy that for now I don't have to get him help. I even tell David how pleased I am that because of his hard work he won't have to go to the special reading group.

Big mistake. Because what will I tell him later when he does have to? Getting help should *never* be demeaning.


Within three months, David is dismissed from the speech therapy program because his speech is judged to be "no longer a handicapping condition," which is a fancy way of saying that because his teacher can now understand him, his articulation is not the school's problem, even though he still can't say the later acquired speech sounds (such as "r" and "th"). The importance of being able to repeat the speech sounds accurately in order to hook them up with written letters is never addressed, because speech and reading are often, mistakenly, addressed separately.

Things go from okay to bad and from bad to worse in class. David's first-grade teacher relies on worksheets, allowing the children to ask for help if they need it. David is shy; he will never ask for help. Unable to work alone, he is lost, withdrawing further and further into himself. How much longer can he throw himself against the unyielding wall of words, solid bricks that offer no entry, no warmth of recognition? No frescoes await behind hidden doors.

In the mornings, David, slouching, eyes averted, stays separate from the other children at the bus stop, trying to disappear into his winter jacket. Often he is crying. Quietly. Charlie Brown, permanent worry wrinkles forming. He begs me to pick him up instead of having to go home with the other children. When a girl who was his friend in kindergarten asks him to read something, he says he is not interested. She calls his bluff. Now he refuses to go to her house. Is *despair* a word used to describe children?

When I ask David's first-grade teacher if he can see the reading specialist, they act as if I am another neurotic, high-achieving mother who is never satisfied with her child ("If you insist, Dr. Weinstein"). At the end-of-the-year conference, the reading specialist calls me in. "You know, Mrs. Siever, he's really not reading."

## Reading with Mom

In the middle of first grade, Mommy went to my teacher and told her I wasn't learning to read. Mommy wanted me to go to the special reading group. My teacher said okay, and I went. I liked the reading specialist a lot in the beginning. We played a lot of games with the letters, and we worked a lot on the vowel sounds, which are really hard because it's hard to hear them. It was specially hard for me because of my speech. I couldn't make the sounds clear, and when I would repeat them in my head they wouldn't sound so clear. Like I couldn't say *school*. When I tried it would come out "ghool" and then I would think it started with G. Like I was trying to see if the word *forgot* made an "er" sound like in *worth* or and "or" sound, but I say *ferget,* so it sounded like "er" to me even though it isn't.

I could tell Mommy was upset. She would try to get me to talk about reading all the time, but I wouldn't. Mommy wanted to be the one to teach me to read. She said so. It was terrible to try and read with her. Mommy tried making up board games for us to do where I'd have to read a few words if I landed on a certain square. Making up the game was fun, but I didn't want to play. Mom would make up charts of words like Lotto, but none of these things helped me. I just felt mad every time I looked at them.

In first grade, Mommy would bring me books to try to read myself. They were the *BOB* books. I hated those books. Anything but the *BOB* books. "Bob sat on the hat. Bob sat on the mat. The cat sat on the mat." Who would want to read stuff like that? It just wasn't interesting. And I couldn't even read it anyway. I just tried to memorize it and say it so Mommy would think I was reading it. I hated the computer program, *Reader Rabbit.* It was so babyish. I hated *Treasure Island* because I couldn't do anything on the computer. It was too hard. I hated the Dr. Seuss books. Mommy was always trying to make me read *The Cat in the Hat* because she loved it when she was little. By the time I could read it, it didn't interest me.

If you can't read, it's terrible to read to your parents. Mommy would say "Just try to read this. You can do it," but then sometimes I couldn't. I'd miss a word and I'd be so frustrated. I'd feel like an idiot—you don't know anything. Mommy would look upset. It was just horrible. Don't ever read to your parents. I still hate reading out loud to Mommy and even more to Dad. I still sometimes miss small words or skip a line. I still use my finger to

point. It's good to read things over. The first time you try
and figure out the words. The second time you try and
figure out what the words are saying. I still don't really
like to read.


## Tutors

Rather than offer times to reach me at the office when talking discretely
might be possible, I always leave my home number when I call potential tutors. This strategy insures that David or Dan will interrupt the
return call with an "emergency." I take the calls surreptitiously, sitting
in my closet or stretching the phone line to the bathroom so David
won't hear the conversation. The bright accusatory lights in the bathroom illuminate my repeating image in the double mirror, reproducing
into infinity, a true inquisition. A typical conversation:

"Hello, is this Lissa Siever?"

"Yes."

"It's Dr. Belanger returning *your* call."

*Already, I'm imposing, forcing my demands on this woman.*

"Yes, the International Dyslexia Association gave me your name.
I have a six-year-old son. I'm . . . well, I'm not really sure that he needs
to see anyone. He was tested at age five and had a color-shape anomia."

"I'm not familiar with that."

"It's when they can't name letters and shapes. It often predicts for
reading problems." *Well, if she doesn't know that how good could she
be?* "He didn't have an overall language problem. He's quite bright,
really. . . . He had speech problems. He's gotten help for his speech,
and it's really improved. He's really a great kid." *Really?*

"Where is he now with his reading?" she replies, trying to get some
straight information.

"Well . . . he knows all his letters and letter sounds."

"Can he rhyme?"

"Yes. He's good at that. Always was."

"That's important. Can he put whole words together?"

"Sometimes. He seems to have sight words. He can read little sentences. He doesn't like to look at books at all. But they're not that worried about him at school. They put him in a resource room group, but only because I insisted. They felt he was doing all right."

"Oh. Well maybe he just needs a little time. Children do tend to read at their own rates, you know. Everyone is different."

I backtrack, more desperate now, realizing I've gone too far in minimizing his problems. "I know he's having difficulty."

She sums up. "I tend to believe mothers. But I really don't have any time. I've got a waiting list of about ten people. Why don't you call in six months and we'll see where we are? He may have made tremendous progress by that time."

*Obviously, she doesn't like me or David. Otherwise she would have had time, she would have bumped us to the top of the list.*

I don't ask her to suggest anyone else. I know I'll never speak to her again. Telling myself that I've done my best (*it's not my fault she doesn't have time; she's booked for years*), it's possible to ignore how I got her to say it was okay to wait.

## Quick Fix

One day I heard Judy tell Mommy that Isabel didn't like to read at the beginning. Judy is Isabel's mother. Isabel is my friend since we were babies. It was hard for her like it was for me. It was a struggle. She used that word. Judy would have to force her to try to read. One day, Judy said, Isabel woke up and she could read everything. It was a foggy day when Judy said that to Mommy. Later, we rode home in the car. We were just going around a curve in the road in the middle of the way home where the road goes away from the reservoir, I said to Mommy, "Will I be able to read in one day, like Isabel?" I saw a Pez dispenser, so we must have gone to the candy store that week. Mommy said that did happen to some kids, but it doesn't happen to everyone. I asked if it would happen to me, and she said she didn't think so.

I felt crushed of most of my confidence, but I still had

a little bit left. I still thought that would happen to me, that I would learn to read in one day. I kept waiting for that to happen to me. I thought that's how all kids learn to read.

So when I was in kindergarten, I would wake up early in the morning. I'd think maybe this would be the day I would just know how to read. Before I called to Mom that I was awake, I'd try to read a word. One new word every day. But I could never do it. So eventually I gave up. I never told anyone. That was in the end of kindergarten and in the beginning of first grade. I wondered what was wrong with me. I still wonder what was wrong that I couldn't learn to read in a day. It makes me really mad

when I see on TV these ads for things like the Phonics Game or Hooked on Phonics. They say things like a kid learned how to read in eight hours from playing the Phonics Game. You can't do that, right? From playing eight hours? It made me think, *Why are these people doing this, giving kids the hope that they could read just like that?* I thought I would be able to read like that, but even when I was in first grade I couldn't even read a word like *sun*. I just looked at every new word and tried to turn it into a word that I knew. I get really angry, because no one can learn to read like that—right?

## Lying

By the end of first grade, David's worksheets have "Great work" or "Excellent" stamped on them. His Level B Phonics Curriculum workbook is filled out correctly. He tries to read me a book they have given him at school. I convince myself that the school's interventions are working.

David waits until the very last day of school to confess. He is so relieved the torture is over.

"Mommy, I copied from the other kids at school. All the time. Otherwise, I never would have gotten my work done. I couldn't do anything."

Blinding tears erupt suddenly, running fast and hot down my cheeks. David has never seen me cry before. Hoping to hide, I kiss the ridge of his cheek; mascara stains my collar.

"Don't cheat David. No. No. I'm not yelling at you. I know you want to do well. But if you cheat no one will be able to know what is wrong. If you cheat you won't get the help you need." Down on my knees now, holding his face in my hands, I hope he will remember the touch, if not the words.

David's chin appears loosely sewn to his chest, a rag clown with no muscle or bone to support him. "But my teacher will be mad at me. Yes she will. She will. She won't write 'Check plus' or 'Super' on my paper. The kids will know I can't read."

"You will read, David. By the middle of third grade. [Please God.] Don't cheat again."

"Don't tell. Don't tell, Mommy. Please. *Ple-ease.*" His head is shaking side to side; his whole body is wheezing. He picks up a pencil to draw. Anything to forget the whole reading thing. "Please. Don't tell. Promise me you won't tell."

"Davy, trust me. I won't lie to you. Mommy knows about reading. You need to learn to read a different way than other kids. It just happens to some smart kids."

In the office, entranced by my own cleverness, I have glibly told parents "Be proud that your child is lying." All children lie. Lying is a developmental advance, a sign that they no longer believe their parents are omniscient and can read their thoughts. It shows they are separate from you.

Today, I see it differently. David has reasons to lie, cheat, and hide. He wants to save himself embarrassment, of course. But with the peculiar illogical heroism of childhood, he also lies to save me from sadness, and from disappointment.

He knows I want him to read.

At the middle and the beginning of first grade, the teacher asked us to read out loud. She wanted us to read little ten- or twelve-page books, and some kids were reading like fifty of them. I only read one, and I was so mad that everybody else read fifty. I only read one book, but I barely read it. I just faked reading the rest because it would look so bad if I only read one. I cheated. I would look at them and use my finger and pretend I was reading. We had little reading groups. Me and four or five other kids lined up in a group. All the other kids would read quick in a few minutes, and it would take me a long time. It was hard. I saw other kids go through quickly, and I was trying to sound out *wh—wh—what* and it would make me feel bad. Like I was stupid.

My teacher said to me, "Some children are good at behaving, and other kids work faster at reading and writing. You are good because you are good behaved and it takes you a little longer to get it right." She was trying to make me feel good, and I did feel okay that I was so good behaved. I was good behaved. I never went to the principal. I was the only one in first grade who didn't go. But I wondered why I was so slow at the other stuff.

In school, in first grade we would do a lot of worksheets. I hated working in my phonics book alone. I just couldn't do it alone. I would look at a word and I would know all the letters, but it was hard to put the sounds together and I was scared to get it wrong. I just wanted to never, never, never look at it again. I'd just try to copy from the other kids. My first-grade teacher scared me. She would yell at the bad kids. I was never bad-behaved. But then the kids who she would yell at would pick on the other kids like me. I was always afraid she would yell at me if I got something wrong. I just started to copy the other kids. When we would have to do work in school, when somebody wasn't looking, I would just look on their paper and see what the answer was to one of the questions. And then if someone said I was copying (some people would call it cheating), I would say "No, I'm not." But I really was. And then sometimes, when I would go up to the drawer where the teacher had all her papers, the kids' papers when they finished them and then she collects them, and I already put mine there, and I take it out and I would try to correct my mistake after cheating it from somebody. I used to feel a little mad, a little happy. A little mad like *Oh, oh what am I gonna do? I'm stupid.* I would worry, *Well, you can't cheat forever.* A little happy, *Phew, not going to the principal's office. I did the paper, phew. It's over for now.* But I knew there would always be tomorrow. Sometimes I'd cry on the mornings Mommy would go to work early and my baby-sitter made me take the bus to school. I'd stand at the bus stop and cry because I didn't want to go to school. But I didn't really want to tell anyone I needed help, either. I thought they wouldn't love me if I wasn't smart and needed help. I saw my parents reading all the time, especially Dad.

I stopped cheating when the work got to be a little easier and Mommy told me I shouldn't cheat. I was going to be okay. I told her after the year was over, in the summer. I just stopped actually. I taught myself to stop. I still want to cheat, but it's getting better. I know that I can do well enough now. I hate to write. Sometimes, Mommy tells me that spelling will really not matter when I grow up. I feel good. But sometimes I think she is just saying that because she's my mother. Maybe I really am slow. Once Mommy was reading the story of Pandora's box. We decided to make up our own sins. I said that my sin was to be slow.

## The Wonderful Mrs. Greene

A take-charge whirlwind, Mrs. Greene, strides in. Disguised as a *very* blond woman in her late 40s, she sports horn-rimmed glasses, black jeans, and a flannel work shirt that somehow look right with incongruously delicate purple ballet flats. A beat up, stuffed to the gills brown leather briefcase is exploding under her arm. Maybe it's her disdain for lengthy introductions, but she seems more Mary Poppins than Glenda the Good Witch. I keep checking for the umbrella, not quite believing she could have arrived in a four-wheel-drive Subaru.

We stand awkwardly in the entry hall.

"You got my name from Matthew's mom?"

"She raved about you. But she didn't tell me much about your qualifications."

"Don't worry. Every child I've ever worked with has learned to read."

So attached to my professional qualifications that my wedding invitation looked more like a new office announcement (*"Dr. Lissa Weinstein and Dr. Larry Siever are proud to announce . . . "*), I am a bit taken aback by Mrs Greene's casual approach.

"Do you want me to introduce you to David? He's shy with strangers."

"Nyah, I'll be fine. I make a good connection with all children. I'll just go right in and say hello. Where is he?"

She finds David crouched behind the family room sofa. I have no idea what she says, but after some coaxing, he agrees to meet with her in my "home office." He only comes out once during the hour and a half evaluation.

Hillary, in her usual bossy older sister mode, is visiting from St. Louis. She is making me throw out hand-me-down clothes that she gave me too many years ago, reorganizing the furniture, and yelling at me to get out of the garden.

"Where does she come from, Lissa?"

"I think she's the head of Special Education in another school district."

"You think? Didn't you ask? With everyone you know in the profession?"

"Do you think I should go listen in at the door?"

Mrs. Greene looks quite serious when she emerges. I imagine her wringing her hands in good-natured frustration at the disorganization, thinking, *Well, these people really need me*. She shows me her evaluation. It's quite sophisticated, breaking down the reading process into its component parts to see precisely where David will need help. She knows what she's doing.

"He doesn't really know his letter-sound associations. He has sight words only on a kindergarten level, and he can't read sentences."

"Oh. Well . . . well I hadn't known it was that bad. Maybe he's just nervous with a new person. He's had a lot of help. I think . . . Well, I've tried to do all sorts of things with him to help him read." I'm babbling. She doesn't cut me short, but she is businesslike.

"What kinds of stuff have you been doing with him?"

I show her the board game David and I made up together. The players do various reading tasks or live through the perils of the Jurassic world. From her effort to suppress a wry smile, I understand why Milton Bradley has not yet called.

Making up the game was fun, but we never play it. Sight word Lotto, another of my creations, lays untouched. David never looks at the words for everyday items taped all over his room, or the list of the first twenty numbers, or my rendering of the addition and subtraction facts, or my rendering of the New York Subway system where the "E family" words live on various train lines.

"He needs to be here," she says, very matter-of-fact. "I usually start twice a week, and we'll see from there. I'll come here to work with him. He's very frightened and wants to hide what he doesn't know. We'll go slow. I always start with what they already have under their belt so they don't feel like a failure from the start."

"What will you do with him? Should I get anything?"

"I pretty much keep my own portable shop. I'll bring what he needs, when I get to know what he's interested in. I start them learning a fixed progression of letter-sound relationships using multi-sensory reinforcement, then move on to consonant blends, vowel sounds, syllables, then whole words." It's a speech she's given before, trying to get intrusive parents to back off. "I do a lot of dictation because writ-

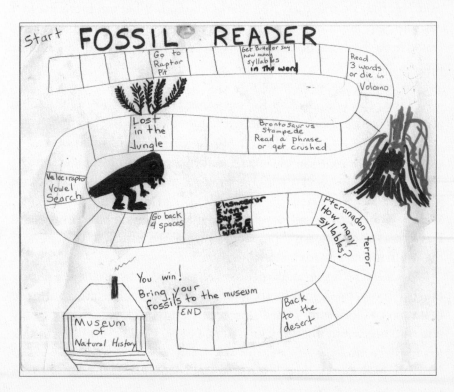

ing the letters helps him learn them. I teach reading, beginning writing, and comprehension together, so they actually learn to read for meaning, not just sound out the letters."

One foot out the door, she says, in lieu of a farewell, "By the way, don't make him read to you. It makes him too anxious."

I don't like her already. She's done nothing to assuage my fears or feed my hope that David doesn't need help. The next time she comes, it's even worse.

"Do you think he'll need a special school?" I ask, again as she is leaving. I'm sure she'll say no.

"I'm not sure yet. I'll let you know."

I cannot stop myself from asking the question so many desperate parents have asked: "Why should this have happened to him?"

"Look, it's his cross to bear. Everyone has something, and he has many gifts."

I spy into the folders she has left in my office that contain the exercises they do together. Red marks abound. What am I looking for?

The next morning, waiting on the camp drop-off line, Hillary asks David how he likes his new tutor. Reflexively, I start to answer for him.

"Well, I'm not so sure about . . ."

"Lissa, can you shut up for once. Let David talk for himself. You are unbelievable. I'm not interested in whether you like her."

"I don't know, Aunt Hillary. She's weird," David replies.

"What's so weird about her?" Hillary hones in on the detail.

"She has fluorescent hair. It's a weird color. Fluorescent. You can spell it. F-L-U-R-S-T."

My God. He's trying to S-P-E-L-L. It's the only time I've ever heard David brave spelling anything longer than three letters. Mrs. Greene is the tutor for me! I won't let fear get in the way.

Mrs. Greene brings me articles on reading processes. They're mostly things I know, but I hold on to them like a talisman, like tangible proof that I'm not alone with David's problems. Maybe David is not the only one who needs a mother. Luckily, Mrs. Greene is always willing to talk to me afterward.

"I think I need a therapist. I just can't handle this. It's so not fair.

He's just a little boy . . ."—things I've said a thousand times, as if saying them one more time will make them vanish.

"Oh, Lissa," she says, gently frustrated. "Everyone feels this way when their kids have problems. Just people can't admit it, so they pull away or try to force their kids to be someone they can't be, or don't let them get help or get paranoid about school." She softens. "I'll hold your hand. It's part of my job to help the parents adjust."

Because he is so self-protective, David is not an easy child. Mrs. Greene works to make him feel safe. She brings him dinosaur bones and has him trace the bones between stints of dictation. There is a lot of repetition in the work that David calls "stupid," but being able to do something easily makes him feel smart. She always lets him have a lot of success before starting something new. Mrs. Greene uses "we" a lot when she talks to David. They are a pair. By borrowing her strength, he will read.

"It's like swimming. You already know how. You just have to practice and learn to get better and better."

David, an incessant complainer, never gripes about Mrs. Greene. "How long will I have to see you?" he asks, his questioning eyes contradicting his showy bravado, betraying a wish that she stay forever.

"I'll be at your Bar Mitzvah. I'll be at your wedding. You'll never get rid of me."

Mrs. Greene saves my son's life. A comrade in arms, we drink endless cups of coffee, discuss reading remediation, and talk about what shoes to buy for fall. In between, we discuss David.

"Your David has a good style. When he's interested in something, he has to know everything about it. Then he moves on. Nothing wrong with that."

I put Sight Word Lotto away. Fossil Reader is retired to the file cabinet. The sensation that I am spinning faster and faster, a planet about to break its orbit, begins slowly to subside. When we go on vacation at the end of the summer, Mrs. Greene offers terse words of advice:

"Leave him alone. Don't try and get him to read. Just enjoy him."

We spend the last two weeks on Cape Cod in a very small cottage watching the tadpoles slowly develop into frogs as school approaches. We catch a few, holding their disgusting, thrilling, slimy bodies for a long minute before throwing them back into the pond. We notice the deep royal blue on the body of a dragonfly, hear it buzz, and watch a bee struggle not to die after it has fallen in the sand by the lake. The last thread of a spider's web evaporates in the morning sunlight, and an egg sac has been left behind. We start slowly on a new trajectory. We are learning to see.

At the end of first grade, Mommy said I should see a reading tutor, because some kids needed to learn to read in a different way than the way they teach it in school. I hated the idea of seeing a reading tutor. I already had so many special helpers. I had my speech lessons twice a week, speech in school and reading group in school, and now this. When would I ever have time to play?

I was mad and scared to see a new reading tutor. I wanted to see the reading teacher from school because I knew her and she made me feel good, but Mommy said that I couldn't because she could only see me in school. I liked the reading group at school because I was with the other kids and my friend, Jonah. I wasn't sure about the new reading tutor. I felt nervous when I first met her. I don't know why. I wanted her to like me, and I thought she wouldn't like me because I might have said something mean.

The first day wasn't so bad because I felt like I was a rich person to have my own tutor. I was wearing a red shirt with jeans and my new sneakers because it was the first day of camp. The first time we had to read some stupid book. I think it was called *Reading Challenges*, and it had a picture of the NFL on it. I was drinking Tang, the kind you make from powder, and I made it very sweet. The third time we looked at a list of words. Now I know they are called sight words—words you just look at and know what they are. She made me do all these things to see if I could hear the sounds in the words. I could hardly do anything. She made me go over and over stuff I thought I knew already. We would do stuff to make me read. We would have to do dictations. Then she made me use those words in a sentence. We would do stories and I would have to read the stories and answer questions about them. She told me I already knew how to read, but that I just needed practice at it.

I kept on trying to read. I knew what all the different cars were called. I could recognize a Toyota or Nissan or a Dodge. Whenever we were in a parking lot and I would see a car that I could recognize, I would say the name over and over and look at the letters on the back of the car that spelled out the name. After a while they began to match up. I tried to say a word in my head when somebody said it. If someone said "Microsoft," I would try to say Mi-cro-so-ft over and over until I could hear the sounds.

Short stuff was better.


### How the Dinosaurs Died Out

Sitting at the kitchen table, David's eyes are clouded, focused on a distant event. He is drawing dinosaurs, passionately filling notebooks with freehand drawings and tracings, copying their names underneath, working hours on end. Each drawing is a story, questions asked and answered, a fantasy made external.


## Lost Lizard

See in the middle that little lizard with the swordfish mouth? He *is* looking for his mother. All the other dinosaurs are trying to keep him away from her. He has a lot of enemies. In the corner are some of his friends, A Pachycepalysaur and an Anklyosaurus. He meets them along the way to talk to. The Icthysaurs are against him. His mother doesn't see him.

I force myself to look. Meat eaters, devouring each other. Prominent hideous teeth. Horns. Spiked feet for ripping flesh. Blood dripping from the mouth after a bite. Small, powerless dinosaurs, tiny hero victims with holes in their sides, looking out of the drawings, plaintive, unprotected, resigned to their fate.

Showing a strong preference for carnivores, David is not interested in the gentle brontosaurus, or the harmless, though well armored, Anklyosaur. Lunging for the soccer ball, he imagines himself a charging Velociraptor. No longer the defenseless, tiny David, he takes what he wants! The warm wetness of his nightly shower becomes the Early Permian world, and David insists he *is* a Dimetredon, forcing his soapy hair straight up into a sail. A Pleiseosaur, with his elongated neck and satisfied smirk, moves gracelessly through swim class. Pterodactyls swoop for prey that look (to me) surprisingly like Dan. The Pachycephalosaur is also a favorite; its ten-inch-thick skull offers solid protection for a vulnerable brain.

We own many books on dinosaurs, leftovers from Larry's childhood and mine, but David insists on the latest information. So what if the books are repetitive? Anything with a letter is okay by me. I follow the lead of his obsessive interests, reading to him about the dinosaurs. Day after day. Night after night. We hang a poster that separates the dinosaurs into different periods and classes and make an elaborate diorama, "Land of the Dinosaurs," using our entire collection of plastic dinosaurs and "boulders" from the garden. We bake dinosaur cookies. David writes his ideas about the dinosaurs in invented spelling:

"Tkhe ditwdon was no a dinsor. It was a pelicosor it wotck on all for it had a dosol fin fortck on its bak the fqucysefolesoris had a Big Dom on its hed with was 10incthick which he ust maby for beyingledr of the hord are mating consest the sponsors lokt insacley lock ditrodon sponsoros had lots instserinsors sharp teecht for caching fish Wuck on 6 feet the end these are my favrein DINOSAURS"

[The dimetrodon was not a dinosaur. It was a pelicosaur. It walked on all four feet. It had a dorsal fin perched on its back. The pachycephalysaur had a big dome on its head which was ten inches thick which he used maybe for being leader of the horde or mating contests. The spinosaurus looked exactly like the dimetrodon. Spinosaurs had lots of spines and rows of little sharp teeth for catching fish. It walked on all six feet. The end. These are my favorite dinosaurs.]

Maybe no seven-year-old should be able to spell such large words. True enough. What marked David as dyslexic was that he couldn't spell "the" correctly.

How did the dinosaurs die out? David's answer:

"I Thick i gigNit SaNdStom came and covrd evry Dinoarus and they cold not dreth Maby the Mete etr to dover and the mete eta had noning to et Mebe a gigti tido wav kom."

[I think a gigantic sandstorm came and covered every dinosaur and they could not breathe. Maybe the meat eaters took over and the meat eaters had nothing to eat. Maybe a gigantic tidal wave came.]

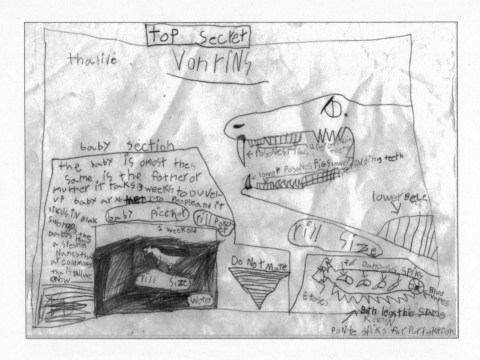

Nobody really knows for sure how it happened. But somehow, David starts to read. Not a lot. Certainly not for pleasure. But enough, enough to know that he will read.

One day David is working very, very hard on his drawing of a dinosaur skeleton.

"Mommy, look. These are the original pieces, and these are the parts that the scientists made from molds. A lot of pieces were missing, but the scientists managed to fix the skeleton and make the whole dinosaur over the way he should have been."

Just as he begins to read, David's curiosity takes off. Compared to my friend's children, he never asked a lot of questions about sex. Now, he wants to know! If he can break the code of reading, why not solve the other great mysteries? His questions are voracious. "How are babies made?" "How do they come out?" "Why are girls made different than boys?" "What do girls have?" "Is that all they've got?" "How did you and Daddy make me?" "How will I grow big like Dad?"

David works assiduously on a mock museum exhibit of a new dinosaur species: Von Rins.

Translation:
Baby Section (Baby Picture, Real Picture): The baby is almost the same as the father or mother. It takes three weeks to develop. Babies are no threat to people, and it lives in black swamps. Babies have a special name that is Coldmongus. That is all we know.

Inside the mouth of the adult Von Rin are poisonous fangs, upper peregrinating teeth, lower poisonous fangs, and lower grinding teeth. The picture of the leg shows four dangerous spikes, blood veins, and pointy spikes for protection. It's still a dangerous world.

David is careful to note "Do Not Mate." One little brother has been enough for him.

I was really interested in the dinosaurs. I would draw and trace them over and over. I could recognize all the different dinosaurs. It turned out that my tutor also liked the dinosaurs. She had even gone on a fossil dig in Montana. She once brought me a bone. She brought books we would read together on the dinosaurs. That was a lot better than the storybooks. I still don't really like storybooks. I like to learn facts. I was always happy to talk with her about new dinosaur facts. We talked a lot when they found that new bird dinosaur.

Mom and me would go to the Museum of Natural History and we got some dinosaur posters that had all the different types and their pictures. We already had a lot of little plastic dinosaur toys so we made a diorama in a shoe box called Land of the Dinos. Mom painted the background and we poured a big glue lake and poured blue sand on it. We got some dinosaur cookie cutters and made lots of sugar cookies.

I got a deck of dinosaur cards from Grandma Dorsi. There was a description of each dinosaur under the picture. Some books mostly had just pages of information and no pictures. I liked the books more with the pictures. There would only be a little written on each dinosaur. After a while I started to do the same thing that I did with the car names. It was also really easy to recognize the dinosaur names. They were long. You couldn't mix them up with other words. There aren't many other words that look like "Plesiosaur" and have a picture of a sea dinosaur next to them. I had to do a report for school on a dinosaur. I chose Heterodontosaurus. It was an uncommon dinosaur, but it was in most dinosaur books. It had grinding teeth for plants, but it also had sharp teeth for chewing meat. It was mostly a plant eater, but it would defend itself if it had to. I liked that. I was the only one in the elementary school to pick that dinosaur.

So I could recognize the big words. I didn't have to read them or sound them out. I looked at them and looked at them. One day, I could sound them out, too. My teacher used to say, "Sound it out," when I couldn't read a word in school. But I couldn't then. Didn't she get it? If I could have, I would have. But now I started to try to sound out the little bits of information in the small paragraphs or the back of my deck of dinosaur cards.

I loved the dinosaurs. I thought they were cool. They didn't have problems. They were big and tough and I just liked them. I really wanted to learn about them, so I kept looking and looking at the words. That's one thing I can tell other kids who are having trouble learning to read. Find something you want to learn about. Otherwise it's just too hard to read.

# Chapter 8

# Second Grade

## Self-Portrait

First Day of Second Grade

I am sweating because I am working so hard.

Written in David's second-grade journal:

*It wus okit gym most ov the time Mr Sterling toking abor-saty and then we did fitnis and ten we lft ithink i had a good fost day.*

[It was okay. It was gym most of the time. Mr. Sterling talked about safety and then we did fitness and then we left. I think I had a good first day.]

*Mr. Lupa the art teacher said he didn't think I was being serious with my picture, but I said that is how I felt. He didn't let me use it in the art show. But I still kept my first copy.*


## Spelling

After a few days, David's second-grade teacher notices his obvious problems reading, writing letters, and spelling. I am called in for the now expected but still dreaded beginning-of-the-year teacher conference. She tells me he will "of course" (*is there ever an easy "of course" for a parent?*) need remedial help. She asks, "What's wrong with him? Will he grow out of it?" She's not at all mean. In fact, she's a dedicated woman, and David likes her because she doesn't yell. She's just ignorant, puzzled by a child who can express himself verbally but can't master these rote skills. Like the majority of teachers without any special training, she doesn't understand learning disabilities—at all.

*Blah, blah.* "David is quite bright, *blah, blah, blah,* but he has a specific reading disability and trouble with phonetic processing and motor skills, *blah, blah,* which makes writing difficult." She "of course" does not believe he is smart because "of course" children who are smart should be able to read and to write. She believes that he is slow, an opinion he is rapidly coming to have about himself. "Of course" David doesn't really get it, either. Why can't he do those things? Only someone who is stupid can't read and can't spell.

In second grade, children are expected to give up invented spelling and begin to spell conventionally. Usually, children start to alter their own spelling automatically as they become more familiar with print. They go from using a single letter to indicate a whole word, to representing syllables and then realizing that each phoneme is represented. They become increasingly familiar with the way words look and learn common orthographic patterns, getting the "look" of the word as well as the phonetic aspect. Usually . . . but not so with dyslexic children. For them, spelling is a long process, best learned by rules that allow them to generalize the structure of written language.

In second grade, children get spelling tests.

How can I get him out of this? He'll never spell. He can't even copy the words correctly because his handwriting is so bad.

Mrs. Greene is her usual sensible self. "Look, even if you sent him to a special school for kids with learning disabilities, he'll have to spell. You can't always protect him." She suggests alternatives. "Maybe you can tell him he has to spell four of the words correctly. Maybe he can write the words over when the other kids take the test. Let him try. You can't control everything for him. Even if you could there's a world outside your house that he'll have to face."

The first spelling list arrives home. It is impossible, without rhyme or reason. Well, most of the words have the letter "a" in them. However, some use the long a sound and some the short a. The only way to get the list is pure memorization. Even if David could memorize the words for long enough to pass the spelling test, it wouldn't help his spontaneous spelling.

Friday, the day of the test, David hides the results in his homework folder. While I'm putting lunch in his backpack on Monday, a strip of paper falls out.

*My God. The letters, the way he writes them.* A rag-tag army in defeat stares at me, ranks broken, fat colonel capitals walking sadly next to undernourished lowercase privates. His words are uncoordinated, clumsy shapes, tangible representations of the little boy who couldn't do jumping jacks. His body in the letters.

Other shocks follow. Some sounds are omitted completely (*plan* for "plant"), blends such as "fr" or "nk" are particularly difficult (*faend* for "friend," *thac* for "thank"). Whole syllables are lost, vowel sounds are substituted for one another, and he can't be hearing the sequences of sounds in words (*afet* for "after"). David gets one correct, two if you count the q in camq as a backward p, because he doesn't differentiate between letters that are the same shape but written in different directions.

*How can I tell him I've seen the test without making him feel worse?* David walks into the kitchen and catches me staring at the list. His gaze drops to the floor.

"Don't worry David. You did fine. Spelling will take a while. I'm glad you tried." *How can he believe me? He knows how the other kids did. Why must he go through this? It's bad not to perform well, a constant reminder he is all the things children hate—small, powerless. The letters, black gnats, metamorphose; turning into butterflies, they spread colorful wings and fly off the page, freeing us from our limitations, leaving white space behind.*

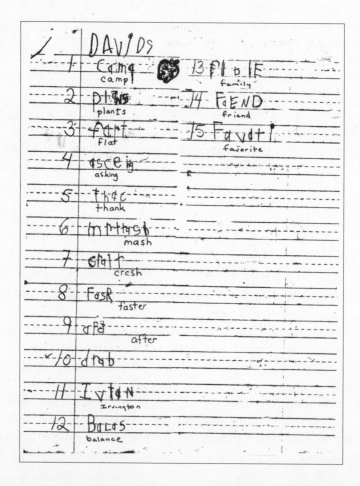

At soccer, a mother tells me her daughter got all fifteen words right. "It's unbelievable how hard she worked. I *never* thought she could do it." Her exaggerated amazement poorly disguises her bragging. "How did David do?"

I drop in the tape and click Play . . . "David has a learning disability. He can barely read, so spelling is out of the question."

There is a long pause before she brushes her hair off her forehead and touches my arm with all the sincerity of trite condolence. "Well, as long as he is happy. Look at him playing. That's what really matters." She is thinking *Not me, not my child*. Who can blame her?

She no longer makes overtures for our children to become friends. In the eyes of other parents, he will become a less high status child, dropped from the group of "smart" and valued children.

I will never be really friendly to this woman again. Even worse (I will feel ashamed for this later), I'm angry at David for making me feel as awkward as the gawky bespectacled too-tall thirteen-year-old I once was. How did I get back in the schoolyard again?

David's grade on the first spelling test lands him with the reading teacher. On her lists, there is a relationship between the words chosen. David learns to sound out the words and to understand each week's rule. He does well even without a lot of studying. He feels proud.

I am a boy who gets 100 on my spelling test,
I wonder if I could travel back to the Jurassic Period,
I see the TV as I watch a different show,
I want to get a toy every second day,
I am a boy who gets 100 on my spelling test.

I pretend my brother and I play and I am the captain,
I imagine what I am doing a few days later,
I feel quite good now but not the best,
I know the summer will come,
I cry when I don't get a toy,
I am a boy who gets 100 on my spelling test.

I know most everything about dinosaurs,
I *say* the *Star Wars* video,
I dream about *Star Wars* the movie,

I try to lift up my brother,
I hope I will get the deluxe Star War set,
I am a boy who gets 100 on my spelling test.

Poem describing himself: Middle of second grade

"F-U-C-K, That's fuck. I can spell that correctly." David takes a moment to view his handiwork on the thirty Post-it notes he's using to decorate the kitchen instead of doing his homework. There are other words too, like B-I-T-C-H and S-H-I-T. They *are* all spelled correctly, with the exception of K-I-K MY A-S-S. It's a pity, because *kick* is one of his spelling words.

"Why can you spell all the curse words right, David?"

"It's easy. You can sound them out."

That can't be correct. Because by any logic, if you can spell *fuck* with its silent "c," you should be able to put that same "c" in kick. If you can spell *bitch* the right way, you shouldn't be spelling *witch* as "witz." So what is it?

Dirty words are E-X-C-I-T-I-N-G. David likes to write them, say them over and over, and look at them. The thrill gets him past his wish not to see and his difficulty memorizing. Eventually, he could be taught to connect *bitch* and *witch*.

Dirty words. Teach my David to spell using dirty words? Words I try to get him not to say in public? Pretty proper in my professional demeanor, a bit of a priss, really, I imagine the whispers of the soccer moms:

"She taught him—what?"

"He said—that?"

But what can I say? I say the H-E-L-L with spelling lists. G-O-D D-A-M-N, David, do you hear that silent "n"?

## Classification

The members of the Committee on Special Education are already seated in a semicircular formation when Larry and I enter the room.

Our places are conspicuously empty, the places where the accused will sit. We are surrounded on both sides. I tremble slightly.

The District Head opens the meeting by reviewing the reasons David has been referred to the Committee. It's a well-used script. The documents I have given the school—the neuropsychological evaluation, the speech evaluation, and the occupational therapy evaluation—are distributed. "Let's talk to the teachers first."

David's second-grade teacher begins. "Well, in the classroom, I feel his reading is improving. He is able to read out loud to the other children and seems to look forward to doing that." The reading remediation teacher, nodding, concurs. "However," David's teacher continues prissily, "I'm concerned about his writing. I look at how he's writing, and I'm concerned about how he will do in third grade, when they expect you to be able to write independently. Perhaps he should be moved to a self-enclosed classroom where he'll be able to get more help."

*Yeah. Right. They're failing with him, so they suggest a Special Education classroom. But once he's in there, there's no standards for him or them. They can't fail. No way.*

The teacher has brought David's journal. When I ask to see samples of his writing, they don't look *so* bad. It's invented spelling of sounded-out words—what educational psychologists call Stage 3 spelling. It shows David can hear the sounds, even if he still can't spell like everyone else. So what . . . ?

*My mother, Pauline, has organized a play group for four-year-olds. The other mothers cluck their tongues. They worry because I don't join the group of children, but instead play by myself and don't talk. I hear them discussing me; they think I am "slow." Pauline says, in a voice that no one would dare contradict, "Lissa will talk when she is ready."*

"David only started reading a few months ago. Why would we expect him to spell conventionally?" I get emphatic, expanding on my theme.

"Writing follows reading in most cases. His errors aren't bizarre or random; they show he understands letter-sound relationships. It's an incredible improvement from the beginning of the year. What do you think?" I say, shoving his work at the school psychologist.

The school psychologist takes another look at David's journal and agrees with me. *But what if I wasn't Dr. Weinstein? Would she have spoken against her colleagues if I didn't know enough to argue?*

David's teacher continues, "I'm worried about his math. He doesn't know his math facts. He doesn't know coins and place value. Maybe he also has a math disability."

The suggestion of a "math disability" irks me. Beginning math is a language. The memorization of math facts is no different than remembering any other piece of language, only a little harder, because words make sense in context. There are rules to how the letters go together, like you don't have b and t next to each other without a vowel between them. But the meaning of a number varies depending on its place value. A child with word retrieval problems will also have a tough time being able to retrieve math facts—they might know that two plus two might equal four, but they might say five or seven. It looks like the child doesn't understand math, even if they get the concept.

I'm on a roll, my courage bolstered by David starting to read, a protective mother Maiasaurus returning to the nest only to find her eggs eaten by some thoughtless Oviraptor. A less-than-appealing combination of rage and eloquence, I puff up to full professorial stature and start my lecture. "The way to tell if a child really has a math disability is to look at the underlying processing necessary for math. Math is really a spatial skill—you have to understand what piece of the pie you are cutting. So you might try to see if he understands one-to-one correspondence, or concepts like bigger and smaller, or if he can tell direction."

Larry and the committee members are eyeing me warily. I move in for the final volley. "David has excellent spatial skills. He does not have a math disability. Period. All children with the kind of reading problems he has have difficulty with early math. It will take care of itself. In the meantime, try writing down the order of the operations for him."

At least this time, for the first time, I have fought for him. Swayed by my logic or worn down by my pedantry, I'll never know—the committee decides to wait on the self-enclosed classroom. Larry and I leave the meeting.

"What do you think?" he asks.

"They hate us. But so what? I know what's right for him. I'm not going to let him be pushed around. The way the whole committee sits facing you. Like you're a child called in for bad behavior. It's intimidating to me, and I do this for other people all the time. What do they manage to do to mothers who don't feel they can trust what they know about their children?"

My valor is short lived. By the time Larry and I part, I'm crying in the car. *Why do you always think they'll tell you he is doing great? Because he's reading and it was such a struggle for him. Can't they see that?*

But the issue of classification can't be avoided forever. David is still classified as having a physically handicapping condition and receives services under that rubric. Now, he'll have to be classified as Learning Disabled. Of course he *is* Learning Disabled, but the issue of classification becomes quite a stumbling block.

I am for classification. If we try to conceal the problem, David will get the message that there is something to be embarrassed about. He will be forced to lie—to others and to himself. He will need special accommodations on standardized tests. His scanning problems will make it hard for him to correctly fill in the bubbles on computer forms, and he could easily mess up the order, even if he knew the right answers. He'll need additional time, because he's always going to read slowly. I want to make sure there is a documented history because accommodations are becoming harder to get. Besides, it was the school that suggested classification. We couldn't have kept his problems secret anyway.

That afternoon, Larry's parents call. I mention that David will be classified as Learning Disabled. The next morning, I receive a second call.

"Lissa." Larry's mother hesitates. She's a diplomat, a former nursery school director who carefully considers and articulates each word. "We have been thinking. We really don't think you should classify David."

*Did I ask?*

"His teachers will be prejudiced against him. He'll never get away from the stigma. He won't be able to go to a good school." Hearing my silence, and knowing what an extended silence might mean, she continues, more gently, "I'm just trying to figure out what will be best for him. I'm concerned."

*Does she think I'm not? God, these people are educated. They are educators themselves. If they feel that people will be prejudiced because he has LD, what hope is there?*

I get off the phone quickly and dial Larry. He makes the mistake of saying, "Maybe my mother feels you are just angry at David. She's worried that classifying him is your way of punishing him indirectly."

I hang up in a rage, hoping to punish Larry directly. Reaching for the Yellow Pages, I quickly thumb to Lawyers: Specialty: Divorce.

By the next day, everyone has calmed down. Larry's parents have talked to several of their friends and agree that disclosure is best. His mother apologetically admits, "I never had these kinds of problems with my children." *Well, I'm happy for her. Is she saying it's my fault? No, probably just admitting ignorance. Sometimes I am angry at him, but classifying him wasn't about that.*

Without classification, there will be no protection for David at school. It's a recipe for failure. He will be made to adjust to standards he cannot possibly meet. The risk of classification is that David will be subject to teasing by other children, who notice that he is being taken to special classes. They will call him "an ED," the cruel nickname for Special Education students.

There *is* one other possibility. A special school for learning disabilities. David could go for a few years, get taught using an approach tailored to his processing problems, then return to a mainstream school. He wouldn't need so much after-school tutoring. Larry and I enter the city of "What-If?"

"What if he's being taught the wrong way at school?"

"What if he'll never catch up?"

"What if we are keeping him from learning with the best teachers around?"

"What if we are just too embarrassed to do the right thing, if this is really about us and not him. Like if we sent him, then he'd really be dyslexic?"

Each "what-if" begets its opposite, a serpent eating its own tail.

"What if we are forcing him to feel different?"

"What if we take him out of the community and he hates us?"

"What if it's not necessary?"

Doing and undoing, turning the stove off and on and off again, trying to be sure we haven't started a fire.

"What if I was Dr. Weinstein, talking to a parent who came for help? Would I tell another mother to put her child in a special school? That she was fooling herself if she didn't?"

Answers are so easy when it is not your own child. Dizzied by our trip down the rabbit hole, we turn to Mrs. Greene.

"I don't really think so. Not now. He's made a lot of progress with the reading. He's just starting to write. What do they expect?" As usual, her words soothe and mollify. "The math and the writing always take longer—until the fifth grade or so." Straight to the heart of the matter, she continues, "You have to think of the whole child. David will take it as a blow. He'll think he failed at reading and you're disappointed."

We ask David.

"No. No. Never. Absolutely not. A whole new faraway school. I don't want to meet a lot of new kids. I don't want to go on a bus far away. Those kids won't live near me. Who will I play with? Will Jonah go? I'll go maybe if Jonah goes."

That night, David is looking over a "book" he made in the first grade. When he falls asleep, I read it.

## The Talking Food

I see a boy with only a hamburger for a friend, so worried about his teeth and his speech that he fears no one will like him.

When he wrote the book, David had an imaginary friend, Cheerio. Cheerio had a brother about Dan's age, with blond hair and a "nice smile" like David's precious friend Connell, who he lost when we left New York. He was (unlike David at the time) "very cheery." David would pretend to talk to Cheerio on the telephone or play games with

ONCE UPON A TIME, THERE WAS A BOY NAMED
JOEY WHO ALWAYS LIKED TO EAT A LOT.

ONE DAY, JOEY HEARD SOMEONE TALKING TO HIM
BUT THERE WAS NO ONE IN THE HOUSE.

JOEY WAS EATING LUNCH.  HE HEARD SOME NOISE
AND LOOKED AT HIS PLATE OF FOOD.  JOEY WONDERED
IF THE FOOD WAS TALKING.  IT WAS THE HAMBURGER!

3

IT SAID, "HEY, DON'T EAT ME." SOON, JOEY
AND THE HAMBURGER BECAME BEST FRIENDS.

THEY PLAYED HIDE AND SEEK, CATCH THE HAMBURGER,
AND HAMBURGER CHECKERS.  FROM THEN ON, JOEY ALWAYS
CHECKED HIS FOOD TO SEE IF IT WAS TALKING BEFORE
HE ATE IT.

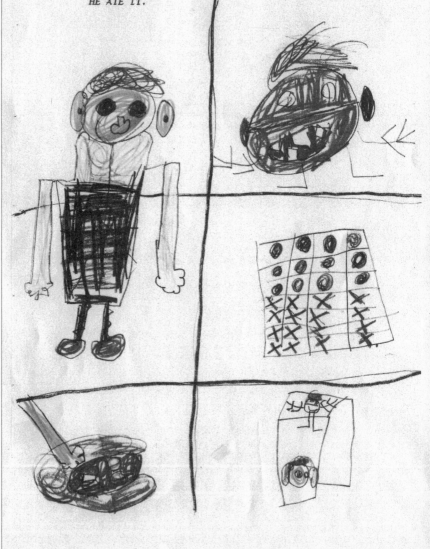

his "automatic friend." Now David has a real best friend, Jonah. They are a funny pair, superficially hard to picture as buddies. Jonah is strong, a natural athlete, a handsome and easily social child. But he, too, had trouble reading and has felt alone. When David accused Jonah of making fun of his speech, Jonah replied "I would *never* do that, David," his heartfelt empathy a reminder of how children are protective yet honest, in ways that adults are not.

I will not send David away.

## Mapping the World: From North Delirium to Montana

Slowly the dinosaurs pass into oblivion. On visits to the museum, we stop at the Hall of Mammalian Evolution to see these less foreign forms, ungulates, giant sloths, wooly mammoths. But these don't hold David in thrall. David is reading. Having joined modern civilization, he looks back with scorn at the world before it became bounded by words. But how is this new world organized?

Maps of imaginary countries begin to replace the dinosaur drawings. In the biblical maps of medieval mappae mundi (the cloths of the world), Jerusalem forms the center of a flower of faith, with Europe, Asia, North America, and Africa splayed around like daisy petals; the Red Sea is painted red. David's maps, too, are pictures of what's important to him; their rebuslike visual language describes his emotional reality. They serve as a tool to examine and codify his place in the world. Literally maps of the mind, they are often shaped like brains; rivers take the place of unidentified sulci.

The names of these imaginary lands are just as violent as the dinosaur drawings, but now the anger exists in the contained form of written words. One island, Villonkilland (Villain Kill Land), is surrounded by Squem Oshen (Scream Ocean). There are dots for the larger cities such as Menkil (Men Kill) and stars for the capitals such as Holikow (Holy Cow!).

Over time, the maps start to resemble what one would see in an atlas, incorporating locations, geographic features, and facts about the countries. The presence of lakes and mountains attest to his attempts to understand a more realistic topography. The drawings describe a life with toys, parks, and hopeful mottoes, a life not unlike his.

The stat flawer (state flower) appears to be a meat-eating Venus's-flytrap. There is a stat tree (state tree) called micro and a stat bard (state bird), a predatory creature not fully evolved from the dinosaurs. The state capital is storelow (a toy store with a small inventory?). The major industries of North Derilem are guns, toys, moshings (guns, toys, machines). The crops are corn, wodermelon, and caruts (corn, watermelon, and carrots), which are his current favorites. The state nickname is mushin (mission) state. There is even a "nashunal park," and at the bottom a small map showing North Derilem's location in the

### North Derilem (North Delerium)
### The Mushin (Mission) State
### State motto: Never Give Up and Stay with It

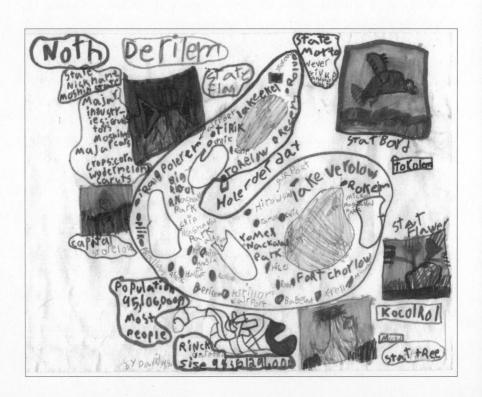

larger country. David wants his state to have "what every state should have."

Last year, David wouldn't write a sentence of more than four words or add his last name to his homework. Now, with the pleasure of a god, he invents names for the features of his countries. The names are always phonetically regular—they are spelled like they sound. Because he creates them, they can't be spelled wrong. No mistakes, no anxiety, but a lot of practice and repetition. *It's unbelievable. He is teaching himself through his play.*

Through the names on the maps, David begins to make more automatic connections between sounds and their written symbols, including the vowels (which are harder because their sound changes depending on the context and the other letters around them). His spelling, although not conventionally correct, is no longer bizarre. It's possible to tell what he wants to say easily . . . much more easily. Good enough for spell check.

With the maps, David advances to a new level. Reading involves taking in the words, but writing requires output. The vivid color of the maps, their patterns, and the graphomotor involvement in writing help David recognize whole words and how the parts of words we call syllables fit together, just like highlighting helps older children remember what they read.

David confuses left and right, which is why he can't tell "b" from "d," which are shaped identically but face opposite directions. Shape and direction are represented in different places in the brain, so some children get only the configuration of the letter, ignoring its direction. Most children start to draw on the left-hand side of a page, just as they read. David's drawings have clustered on the right. With the maps, his drawings become more centered as he uses the compass to orient himself. He stops making so many reversals of letters when reading and writing.

As he begins to write and spell phonetically, David's interest shifts to real maps. Now the world is measured not only by his own imaginings, but by objective longitudes and latitudes. David will join this world, not live on a globe of his own fantastic making, a place where he doesn't have these problems.

When his third-grade class starts learning about states, David picks Montana as "his state" because there is a baby Hadrosaur skeleton in the paleontology museum. He likes "states," and decides to learn all their capitals, birds, and flags. He practices putting together an old wood puzzle of the United States. A Rand McNally map, ignored when it was hung on the wall years before, is used to plan routes across the country. We test the good-heartedness of AAA in our efforts to get from "here to there," gathering free road maps for imaginary journeys. During summer vacation, David insists on touching a car from every state. He starts memorizing world capitals and, to our horror, tests the waiters in Cape Cod restaurants.

How does he remember all this stuff? Despite his retrieval problems, he seems able to retain more of this information than other kids his age. One day I see David biting Finn Crisp crackers into odd shapes. "What are you doing?"

"I'm making state crackers. Look, this one is Idaho. Here's Texas."

They are amazingly accurate. "How do you do that? I couldn't do it."

"Easy. I can remember exactly how the state looks. In school, I 'put' what I want to remember either like a picture or something written inside the state and I see it there."

The facts are organized spatially for him, on the map. No need for the arduous creation of linguistic categories.

David, who still cannot consistently remember whether his older cousin is called Joseph or Alex, does so well in social studies that his teacher puts him on the geography team. People start to compliment him on his good memory. Even though his team does not win, David tells me: "Finally, I feel like I'm worth something."

"The important thing about David is that he loves geography. David's friends are Isabel, Jonah, and Connell. His favorite thing to do is to go to the toy store. David has no pets. He has a brother named Dan. David has about 160 toys and 5 maps and 1 globe. He used to have sea monkeys and caterpillars, but they all died. David really wants to go to Montana. His favorite foods are sushi, lobster, and Burger King. David loves art and he loves the Nickelozone and *Star Wars.* But, the important thing about David is that he loves geography."

David             Self-description: Beginning of third grade

**PART IV**

Letters from Kansas

# Chapter 9

# David and Dan

### Two Guys At War
#### "The Small one is all cut up" Dan: Age 5 ½

"Can we have some alone time, Mom?"

"Dave, I'm kind of busy now. I've got to write and get your Halloween costume ready for tonight."

"You never have time. You spend all your time putting on perfume and makeup. I want to show you my city. It'll just be a second."

*Is there ever enough time?*

The Playmobil city is taking over our basement. The Museum of Natural History, its elaborate entrance modeled after the face of a pig, snakes around the treadmill. Behind, smaller compartments represent the dinosaur halls of different periods and lead into the Hall of Mammalian Evolution, where perverse polyglot animals reside, a cow with the horns of a ram, a dog with the head of a man. Outside, colorful plastic friends greet each other before entering. Thomas the Tank Engine will get you to the museum on Brio train tracks. Near the museum are Lego block restaurants, apartment buildings and Central Park, recreated from Larry's Lionel train setups. David's constructions are complex, with a visual logic that's often hard for my symmetrically ordered brain to "get."

He has been working on this project all week, his devotion fueled by the sting of Jonah's remark that "he talks about states too much." David is puzzled; he doesn't know why he has to force people to see him as smart.

"Do you like it? You see the way I built the restaurant? You can see the little stairs if you want to go to the second level for a party. See the museum. Jonah built that animal exhibit over there, but no one's going to see it. Do you like the restaurant, *really?*"

Dan clumps down the stairs, back from soccer practice. "It was breat," he offers before being asked. Dan's excitement runs shivers through his body. His enthusiastic charm lets us forget that he, too, has some speech problems.

David looks up, irritated. "Soccer is for babies, Dan."

Soccer was no fun for David. Afraid of being hurt, he'd run fast, then slow to a near halt as he approached the pack of writhing seven-year-olds. On defense, he stood stock-still, creating shadow puppets. The bees, mistaking him for a shrub in his green uniform, stung viciously. Dan's thrill pushes the thorns deeper into David's side.

Dan comes over. "Can I help, David? I could help." With the sincere adulation of a younger brother, he wants to do what David does.

"You can't play with the Legos, Dan."

This refusal is not a matter of scarcity. We have several thousand Legos in a trough, a gift from their cousin when he outgrew them.

Dan starts to cry. "David never lets me do anything." He throws himself on the floor, using his younger child's prerogative to inspire guilt and arouse maternal sympathy.

"You're such a cry baby, cry baby Dan," smirks David, knowing he has once again driven Dan to near insanity without even touching him. "You don't really want to play with the Legos. You're no good at them. You can't even follow the instructions."

"I'll make my own cars, David. You could use them in the parking lot." Dan is not buying David's nefarious attempt to get him to submit. David tries another tack.

"You can play with the Battle Squads."

"Okay." Dan, agreeable as always, is grateful to have won some consolation. "Where are they?"

"Oh, I don't know. How should I know?" David shrugs, triumphant, sure he'll get away with tormenting his brother without being blamed for any overt violence.

"I can't find them," wails a distraught Dan.

David loads the cannon for the final decisive strike in this ongoing war. "That's because you are stupid and so annoying. You are really stupid."

My sudden anger at David is a wave and I am paralyzed, small before it, unable to judge whether I should jump or dive under until it passes. I jump and fail, unable to rise above it and under and under and around until I don't know anymore which way is up and where the big hand to pull me up out of the water is. Where is Larry? *Black is back. Where is Brown? Mr. Brown is out of town. Thank you, Dr. Seuss.*

Dan's crying forces me to cope. I go to separate them. "David, come sit with me for a while. Over here. Leave Dan alone." Sometimes physical touch allows David to borrow a sense of control from me. If he feels more special, he might leave Dan alone. But David senses the emotional betrayal of my sympathy for Dan.

"I hate you, Dan. I really do."

"David, cut it out," I snap, not even bothering to hide my irritation. "No you don't."

"I do. I do. It's the truth. You said to tell the truth. I hated Daniel from the moment he was born. I remember the day I walked to the hospital and the baseball game was on the TV in your room. Daniel looked like a cross between a goblin and a hippopotamus."

Dan eyes grow wide with confusion at his brother's betrayal.

*How can David be so heartless?*

The situation quickly regresses. I'm pulling/pushing David into my office for a "talk." "Oh no, not another talk." David's words remind me that even understanding can be used to torment. Perhaps a quick spanking would be less punitive. I trot out my armamentarium of empty threats:

"You're not going trick-or-treating . . . No more allowance if you keep torturing him . . . I'm taking away all the Legos."

*Is this how he feels? Powerless, impotent, a fool? He's made me this.*

David doesn't respond. His refusal to submit plunges me deeper into this orgy of anger. It will leave us both unsatisfied, hating ourselves more than ever. Cold creeps up my legs, tightening my stomach. Spasms of rage pour from my mouth.

"You're just jealous about the soccer, because it was so hard for you . . . Just because you feel stupid in school, that's no reason to call him stupid . . . It's not true that you can't learn. You just have no discipline. You just want everything to come easily. Well, it won't. You'll have to work harder at things . . . You *are* an idiot."

I recognize David's dull-eyed stare as my own, the one I'd hide behind while Pauline lectured me and I was a million miles away, a princess in a kingdom of no pain.

David's defense cracks. He starts to cry. "I'm stupid. That's what learning disabled is. It's stupid. You learn differently. Yeah, you learn the stupid way. The retard way."

Dan jumps in, ever David's champion. "David deserves to get whatever he wants. I don't like it when you yell at David. You have to talk to him really nice. So he'll be nice to me. And I care about him a lot. I care about him so much. It was all my fault what happened."

Dan accepts the blame readily. He feels bad that he can do what David cannot. At the same time, he's jealous of the attention David gets for his problems.

Wistful, Dan tells me, "You don't too much attention after you're five, unless you got problems. I got a few problems, but they are not such big ones. I got a little speech problem, but it will be over soon."

It's true. He often gets ignored. It's easy to sympathize with Dan, to see him as the good child. He's younger, a natural prey. But to David, Dan is an interloper. Dan's decency and charm are all the more painful because David's own thorns only stop hurting when he is cruel to someone else.

## Dan Reading

Peeking in on Dan after bedtime, I find his light on. He is sitting up with a book, mouthing the words to himself.

"Dan, are you reading?"

Dan shoves *Snug House, Bug House* under the bed quicker than an adolescent caught with his first *Playboy*. From his "No Mom. No!" it is clear I should not ask again.

*He's hiding because he's afraid it will hurt David that he can read. Poor Dan. He'll never get to enjoy our pleasure in him without feeling guilty. Thank God they are far enough apart that he won't read better than David.*

I should have known. It was obvious Dan didn't have the same difficulties as David. As an infant, he babbled continuously. At his one-year checkup, he screamed, "What is dat?" when his disbelieving pediatrician held a tongue depressor in front of him. It wasn't really language, just mere imitation of sound, but it was startling. Around the same time, when I tried to wean him, he affectionately patted his favorite breast. "Want dat one," he said, boldly refusing the offered bottle. By the age of two he spoke in full sentences and asked questions. Dan could repeat anything: the alphabet song, the Pledge of Allegiance, the entire text of *The Hungry Caterpillar*. He understood rhythm, dancing excitedly to the *Fantasia* video and identifying snatches of its classical music when they came on the radio. Dan was great at those phonics training games you play when you are bored in the car ("If I said 'cat' and I took away the 't' and put in a 'p' instead, what would I say?"). He had no trouble recognizing the letters, learning them easily at 3½ during the great onslaught of David's at-home remediation. Dan was "wired" to read. Larry and I didn't do a *thing*.

The next week we are in the local bookstore, looking for science fiction.

"Is that it?" Dan says, pointing at a sign that reads "ROMANCE."

"Read it."

"RR-OH-MAN-S. Romance!" he shouts excitedly. Romance! He's got it! He starts laughing, his eyes gleam with excitement. Section by section, he tries to sound out all the signs. During the ride home he whispers to himself, "I'm five now, but in ten years, I'll be fifteen. When I'm six, in ten years I'll be sixteen." It's okay to be small now, because he's going to be big soon.

Having figured that out, he asks, "When I go to high school I'll have a girlfriend, right, Mom? And then you'll die."

"Why should I die?"

"Because then I could really love her. Without you being around."

"It's easy," he confides later, trying to teach me how this reading thing is done. "First I look at the letter. Then I sound it out. Then I think of a way it makes more sense. And it's usually right." Dan pauses to make sure I'm getting it. "I don't usually look at the ending sound and the beginning sound and guess one of the words with just those two sounds. I don't usually do that. I look at all the sounds together. Then I match it up with a word I know. I think of a way the sentence will make sense. It always makes sense to me."

He's so proud to break the code. He continues, his cadence slow like the one I used when reading read him *Goodnight Moon* or *Hop on Pop*, paced so I can get every word.

"When I was a little kid I couldn't do it because I didn't know what the sounds of the vowels were. But then I learned them and I could do it. I couldn't do it last year. Then one day I looked at a word—and it was DAD. All of a sudden it was clear. I could see Larry standing right there."

It's so much more than the ability to figure out a word. *He's got it!* He'll read like Daddy. He'll be a grown-up man, able to figure things out. He's part of all those other big people he saw in the bookstore, lounging in big armchairs, sitting at big tables, looking at big words. He won't be excluded forever. It's not just the rote skill of combining the letters into words—it's the whole hookup with a world of words that represent something. Now the world is smaller, more manageable. Things that didn't make sense before are coming into view: The grand relationship between his parents, the scenes of excitement, sadness, sexuality that have been so puzzling are getting restructured with the help of words, narrative, and imagination.

Dan learns to read prices. "It's $9.99, not nine hundred and ninety-nine dollars," he says loud enough so the other customers in Pier One can benefit from his knowledge. When we get home, he dictates a story.

### Bill's Dream

"Bill's mom said, 'It's time to go to bed.' And so Bill went to bed. He fell asleep right away. He was having a dream about—at first he was sad. He had no home, no friends. He was a teenager. He was lost, and he used to have a family but he lost it. He tried to imagine something nicer than what was happening right then in his dream. He wanted to go to a better place, but it was empty in every place that he looked for miles.

"He walks and he thinks he sees something in the distance. When he got close enough to see it really good, it turned out to just be a tree. Then he realized he could make a little house with whatever is around. So he made one. Then he found a little town. In that town he realized what money was. He realized dollars, pennies, nickels, and dimes. Then he started making money for himself. He used to have money but then he lost it, but now he made more and he had some of it. He got some food in town. And he went back to his little home. He found a few friends. They lived a good life together."

Dan can imagine existing without me and Larry. He'll be sad, but he's "realizing" the skills he needs. His pleasure is at the same time a reminder of what David will not have—an easy road to independence, a solid place in the world of men.

## The New View of Self

Fox 5 News. "Today we have Dr. Larry Siever, professor of psychiatry at the Mount Sinai School of Medicine and author of *The New View of Self: How Genes and Neurotransmitters Shape Your Mind, Your Personality, and Your Mental Health.*"

A colleague of Larry's from Mount Sinai Hospital has invited Larry to plug his new book on her TV show.

"How are you today, Dr. Siever? We're glad you could be with us."

"I'm fine, thank you." Larry, a deep-voiced pro at these interviews, looks down modestly. "David! Dan! C'mere. Look. Look. Daddy is on TV!"

"So what?" David replies. "Who gives a crap?" David refuses to move from his drawing.

I adore Larry on TV, his salt-and-pepper beard and beautiful friendly wrinkles around his eyes, a man perpetually rumpled in clothes that only match because I've chosen them. So trustworthy and thoughtful.

It's always good to see your loved ones as others see them. Familiarity breeds . . . How can you idealize someone who yells at you for stealing their toothpaste, or who eats the kids' lunch from the fridge and then denies it? But when I see Lar giving a talk, he looks a lot like Sean Connery. So distinguished, I want him to be my doctor. Or my husband. *My God, he already is my husband.*

Larry is talking about how a child's temperament will shape your treatment of them. PowerPoint bullets are appearing behind him as he speaks. He is talking about "the shy child" in his characteristic cadence, a soothing prosody no matter what he's saying. At home, it drives me insane, but today, joining the community of adoring television viewers, I feel reassured.

"What would you do, Dr. Siever, if your child is excessively shy?"

"Well, you might try to talk to that child in a very even tone of voice."

• **Talk in a calm tone of voice.**

"Research shows that shy children tend to be more autonomically responsive to slight amounts of stimulation."

- **Limit the amount of stimulation.**

"You might try to limit the amount of noise, or the number of children you have over for play dates. It's especially important to set firm disciplinary limits so they feel safe."

- **Set firm limits.**

"That's very interesting, Dr. Siever."

It sounds terrific! I feel better already. I've walked headlong into the perfect life.

My self-satisfied reverie is interrupted by shrieks of excitement. Following David's enthusiastic direction, Dan is leaning over the balcony, dropping eggs wrapped in plastic and Scotch-taped to their stuffed animals. Big Dog, David's favorite childhood bear, doesn't survive the rigid experimental design. His white fur is thick with yolk. So is the entry hall rug, several shoes in the open hall closet, and my coat.

"We're trying to test if they will break."

"Do you want to die young?" I ask, offering some firm limits of my own. Ready to concede that having children is a biological urge worth resisting, I have reached a new nadir in my experience of motherhood, a 4 o'clock in the afternoon of the soul.

*Interesting. Sure. Would Fox 5 like to come over here with a camera?*

Larry calls after the taping is over. "How was I?"

"You were fantastic. I wanted to marry you all over again. But then I looked around the house. You can't believe what's going on. Animal farm. I hope the book can pay for the paint job we'll need. I'm calling Fox 5 and proposing a mini-series: *Personality Experts at Home.* "*Behind the Music*" of psychiatry, but with a very serious Ed Murrow, *This Is Your Life*–type treatment. Maybe it will give us all a new view of self."

**PART V**

To the Emerald City:
Our Journey Continues

# Chapter 10

# New Territory

By the end of second grade, the angry dinosaurs in David's drawings have evolved into machines. Tiny men sit inside, calmly manipulating computers that control the robot animals in battle. The power to fight, the anger that makes one willing to fight and fight to learn, is still not owned. They are still not David.

Jonah is "into" the army. David looks up to his best friend, who is older than him and more physically powerful. Suddenly, David loses his interest in *Star Wars* and the Jedi and stops trying to write admiring letters to George Lucas. Our collection of *Star Wars* action figures, so important, so necessary just a few months earlier now lie untouched in plastic bins. Poor Hans Solo is defeated, David tells me, his "weenie frozen in carbonate." Our AT-AT, fallen over on his side for the last time, awaits potential release from oblivion when Dan reaches the right age.

We start collecting G.I. Joe dolls.

"Not *dolls*, Mom. *Figures*. Girls collect dolls."

Larry and I are veterans of the antiwar movement. Our son interested in the military? Well . . . maybe . . . the Civil War . . . maybe . . . okay. I envision the carnage of Gettysburg reproduced in miniature accuracy in our basement while I read Lincoln's astounding words: "Four score and seven years ago, our fathers brought forth . . ." Me at my mother-teacher best, joining David's worlds, living his fascinations.

This time, however, David doesn't want me. He wants to be with Jonah. This is a boy's game. He wants G.I. Joe figures. All of them. To set up in G.I. Joe Jeeps, to put in G.I. Joe helicopters, to ride on G.I. Joe motorcycles. To dress in their endless variety of military uniforms, complete with their full collection of guns. He wants guns. He wants to make gun noises. *Did I say there would* never *be a gun in my house?* He wants to put on a military helmet and a gas mask. He and Jonah run around the backyard shooting at each other, taking a luckless Dan hostage, or leave the Joes tied and bound to fend for themselves in our garden/jungle.

We buy books: *Tanks, American War Uniforms, World War I, Great Wars, Military Helicopters, U.S. Navy SEALs in Action, SEALs in Vietnam, The World's Great Tanks from 1916 to the Present, The World's Greatest Machine Guns, Airlift, Spy Planes, Bombers, World War II, The Secret War, Pearl Harbor, War Planes, The Scholastic Encyclopedia of the United States at War.*

At the bookstore one day, David insists on buying a book on Nazi war uniforms.

"Absolutely not. Forget it."

"But why, Mom? I already have a book on American Army uniforms. There's British and Russian uniforms in there, too. It's just something I want to learn about. You have no right to tell me what to learn about. I can be curious about anything I want."

"I have family who died in that war. I don't really like war. If you want to know about Nazi war uniforms, you're on your own. Try the library."

"Mom, not everyone is you. You have a set of values. But not everybody has those values. You don't want to kill a living thing. But other people don't feel that way. You can't tell everyone how to feel."

*My son, F. Lee Bailey.*

Some aging military buff, who no doubt also hated his mother, jumps in to defend David. "Smart kid. You have to admit he has a point."

"Oh yeah. Why don't you bring him up? Could you mind your own business?"

Reduced to idiocy in the military book section.

David complains to Larry: "She is so mean. All I wanted was a book. She knows I need to read. How could I have such a mean mother?"

I confide in a colleague. "He's so obnoxious. He's got no other interests besides these war books. There's nothing good about this."

"That's not really true, Lissa. It's a big step forward. All kids are angry. You, Ms. Psychoanalysis, should know that—the old Freud stuff. I want to be powerful like Dad, but I'm small. He could keep drawing pictures of dinosaurs fighting, but drawing isn't so good. You can't do a long story with a drawing. Reading takes you a lot further. You can read about famous battles and weaponry and who started the wars and when and why. You can imagine you are Abe Lincoln or Colin Powell. Learning tames their anger, gives it an acceptable form. And a social form. He's not doing this alone."

"David couldn't do that before?"

"Right. That kind of patterning doesn't occur for kids who don't read easily."

"Ugh. It's gross."

"Don't forget, there are lots of pictures in war books. They reinforce his being able to attach sounds to the letters. Visual input really helps him remember. Back off."

I do back off, but my opinion wouldn't make any difference anyway. David is passionate. A child who couldn't name the days of the week in order now tells me that Pearl Harbor took place on the day after Dan got kicked out of the Children's Center and then he lists the order that each country entered World War II. He knows the names, of guns and important cities in the war, talks about international conflict, starts reading the newspaper, and thinks about how science develops.

The Joes teach us all a lot.

As David learns more about war, the G.I. Joe stories soften. David starts to weave in events from his real life. A visit to the dentist inspires him to brown out Teddy Roosevelt's teeth, proving that even the leader of the Rough Riders, Special Edition Joe and patron saint of the Natural History Museum can suffer tooth decay. Charging the hill behind Jonah's house, Teddy and the Rough Riders are intercepted by Jonah's Golden Retriever and chewed to death.

Larry and I no longer find tortured "figures" laying mummified in masking tape or hung blindfolded from a staircase railing. Instead, David starts to build an army hospital. The hero of this new narrative is a medic. Joes who have been hurt are laid gently on a stretcher. David makes bandages and builds crutches from sticks found in the yard to repair them. Headquarters are created in an old moving crate. The Joes sit around drinking tea and socializing, pausing to stretch backward in a masculine pose, casually confiding tough exploits, and mapping out flight plans. David is as loving to the Joes just as he was to Big Dog at age two, wiping and diapering the stuffed bear as they mastered toilet training together.

Watching the creation of his elaborate setups brings me back to a languid summer when day after day, uncomfortable in the new humidness of my preadolescent body, I made Barbie furniture out of wire hangers and Pauline's leftover curtain material. Sitting on our screen porch, warding off my imminent metamorphosis, my visceral devotion to Barbie's happiness offered a brief respite from the torment of being still-me and not-yet-me. Putting pink slippers with white fur puffs on Barbie's permanently high-heeled feet, I wondered *Will I ever have shoes like that? Or breasts that grow in concentric perfection?* Black-haired from birth, I believed it was possible to grow into a naturally blonde adulthood.

*My God, it's Barbie for boys, a rehearsal for the role of "real guy."*

The Joes come with many accoutrements, extra things to hang off the front of their sculpted bodies—ammunition pouches, binoculars, grenades, knives, guns, water bottles, handcuffs, and helmets. The proportions of their unbelievable biceps and apelike hands and feet would make a real-size man look like a circus freak. But in a boy's hierarchy of value, bigger is better.

A Barbie left at our house (*David would* never *have one!*) enters the games as a character. David has heard of recent attempts to make Barbie more feminist, more "relevant" and gleefully offers tasteless "New Barbie" suggestions: Tollbooth Barbie—a woman who will take your money—and as part of his burgeoning interest in World War II, Concentration Camp Barbie—a woman in uniform.

Barbie's head falls off during some rough play with the G.I. Joes. David holds an egg where the head was.

"She's an egghead," his rising excitement signaling anxiety. He knows "egghead" is a term used for an intellectual.

He smashes the egg hard on the kitchen counter.

"She's brain damaged. She hates her head. Her head is all damaged. It can't be fixed."

"Why couldn't they put him back together again? Why wouldn't they put Humpty Dumpty back again? Why not?" David would ask when he was little. The belief that he is "stupid" for not being able to read fuses with another, less conscious, fear—he is broken, body damaged, brain damaged. Now a new idea joins this core. Girls are weak and broken, missing what boys have. They are the damaged ones. Now to fail at reading is to be feminine, castrated.

*That's why the Joes are endlessly fascinating to him; that's why he has to have them all. He must borrow their big-guy strength to feel powerful—powerful enough to learn. Perhaps the very newest one can help him feel nothing is missing.*

David brings a Navy SEAL and an Infantryman from the family room. "Look at their faces, Lissa. Look. What do you see?"

"They look angry."

"Duh-uh. That shows you don't understand. A little angry, but you can never tell what they are thinking. That's what's important. They are tough, determined. Not surprised or sad. They have poker faces." He pauses to let me examine them more closely.

"Everyone has a scar on the right side. Every one. You know what that says, Lissa? That scar lets you know 'I've been hurt, but I would never, never ever cry even a single tear of self-pity.' "

*Should I cry now or later?*

There is no question about it. G.I. Joes are *manly!* David is talking, talking, talking about getting tough, getting T-O-U-G-H! Asking can he attend a military boarding school and doing push-ups to build his arms. Playing off the military theme, I suggest he make his bed "military style," keep his hair short "military style," and follow orders. No one follows a single one of my orders.

New attitudes emerge.

"You're not the real boss of the house, Mom. Larry is the boss. He's the man." When I try to discipline David, he runs to Larry and says, "Be a man. Tell her to stop." Only partly joking, David now refers to me not as "Mom" or even "Lissa" but uses the simple, generic "Woman."

Suddenly we are separate. His need for help bound us once; now he wants to be in a world where I am no longer in charge. I see myself welcoming, with open arms offering comfort and safety. He sees an octopus, with long, suckered tentacles beckoning. A siren singing, "Come, be weak, be mine again." Faced with his wish to go, I find it hard to do what would be right—stand by and admire, take pleasure in his creations: the intricate setups, the army museums, his stronger body. Instead, I let him stay away a bit too long at Jonah's house. When Larry asks where he is, my voice is bitter. "He really doesn't miss us anymore."

Mothers are made to be left. The wrench of David's wanting to go is sharper than any lost lover; marking a palpable space. A graying emptiness, I'm as unexciting as the G.I. Joe boxes flattened for recycling. What to do now? Streak my hair, flirt with a friend, and reconstitute my body as I knew it before him. I could lose my pregnancy weight. It's only been eight years. My formerly empty vanity is now littered with La Mer skin cream, hair thickener, gel, perfume, twenty shades of brown eye shadow, brushes, rollers, and tweezers. I believed he would always be *my* child. Now I must shift a delicate balance— the child I love as part of me to a child I love as himself.

## The Painted Ladies

Dan has chosen a butterfly garden as his present for finishing the school year. The caterpillar larvae arrive, suffering somewhat in the summer heat in our mailbox, but apparently alive nonetheless. They are larvae of *Vanessa cardui, L.,* more usually known as Painted Ladies, a colorful if common butterfly. Our attempts at growing butterflies from caterpillars caught in the garden have failed; untutored, we left them in the sun and they died. Now we are schooled.

The first week is not so interesting. The larvae eat, get bigger, and start to crawl up to the top of the paper disk. They curl into themselves and begin to hang "head first," resembling corpses suspended in sacks, a miniature insect mortuary. I have to stop Dan from opening the jar and petting them.

"Why not? They are furry. They are probably lonely."

By the end of the week, the Painted Ladies have begun to form chrysalides. Horrified yet fascinated, I am unable to stop watching them, engrossed and partly disgusted, long after the children have lost interest. They hang, fragile and yet indestructible. When you move the jar, they shake, using an ancient method to ward off predators. Four of the five form chrysalides. The last, the smallest larva, seems weak, unable to get to the top of the jar, and is never quite as fat as the others.

"It's the runt," David says.

Eventually, all five hang silently, waiting, changing in ways we can only imagine. The chrysalides become iridescent, goldenly tipped, then darken to protect their inner life. We move them to a box where they will hatch. As with my childhood doll's house, I want to provide the right home. Concerned for their welfare, I arrange rocks, gather twigs, and assess my garden for the right flowers.

One morning, transfixed, I think I see a quick, fierce movement of the wings beneath the crysalide. I call the children. Nothing more happens. Perhaps I have imagined it. We go outside. When we return, a butterfly is hanging there, less beautiful than the pictures on the box and with closed wings. You can see its fake eyes that it uses as camouflage. Its brilliant color is hidden inside.

Dan, ecstatic, tries to place the butterflies in the chains of creation, birth, and death that obsess him.

"I get it—when the baby is kicking he's coming out and he's hatching just like the butterflies. Did I lie there and kick? Did Davy? What about Davy? How did he do it? Except that the babies can't fly. They don't have to use wings, so they cry instead when they come out. That's it!"

We cut flowers and arrange them, deeply satisfied with our efforts if not our results. Dan continues to narrate. "Come on now, come on. He's opening his wings. He's shaking his wings. He's shivering. He's scared. Fly now. When you know how to fly you'll be a butterfly. That's when you'll be a butterfly. Can I touch him? He's a flying flower. He's that beautiful. He's tasting his old friends. Leaves are his old friends, but he still likes them. It's good we gave him leaves, because they are his old foods, cause he still likes them. Fly! Fly! Fly!"

He stops, suddenly. "That one is not flying. He's probably missing his warm cocoon, because he's looking up at it. He's probably thinking how he'd like to go back in. It was warm. Look at him now. He's afraid to close his wings."

Offering them flowers soaked in sugar water, we watch as they unfurl their long, strawlike proboscis and suck up the nectar.

We decided to keep the Painted Ladies a few days. But the observation box was poorly constructed and when one escaped, we set her free. She took off, happily. Excited to see her go, we had done our job—raised them and sent them off. The others got out, too. We found them on the windowsill and coaxed them outside.

All but one. The last Painted Lady had been the smallest caterpillar, slower to climb than the others. She had taken a day more to form her chrysalis, which never quite turned dark and luminous. Maybe she was dead in the chrysalis.

The next day, I found the Painted Lady on the bottom of the cage. The other chrysalides seemed to burst apart, forced open by the urge to live; hers looked as if she had just slipped through. Her wings were folded oddly back on each other, not fully straight like the other newly emerged butterflies. The wings were not merely stuck, but deformed and would never fully extend. She would never fly. When she tried, she would get off the ground a little and then flop, desperately trying to turn herself over again.

Painted Ladies only have a three-week life span. I decide to keep her safe in the box until she dies. She will never know she was different.

"Let's keep her two days and then put her out of her misery," David says, quickly losing interest in caring for something he perceives as defective. "Let's dissect her to see what we can learn."

But I feed the Painted Lady every day, cutting new flowers from the garden, swishing them in sugar water so she had plenty to eat, just in case she would ever be strong enough to fly. I worked hard to make a natural environment, "a habitat" as Dan called it. Sorry that the others had been let go, I didn't want her to be lonely.

There was an urge to prod her wings. First to see if I could stimulate them to move, but later, maybe just to be cruel.

"Do you know what she is doing when she is frightened?" Dan says. She's trying to straighten out her wings so she can fly away. They are a little better than yesterday. Her face is funny. It's got a point on the front. She has dots on her antennae. Maybe she'll lay a lot of eggs."

It was true. She had a face that looked almost devilish, with strange eyes. They say the Painted Lady has 10,000 of them. She looked right at you.

One day she escaped. We found her on the floor of the dining room, still alive. She wanted to go out to the garden. She couldn't move. Couldn't move well. Running quickly to the garden, I grab my most colorful flowers—marigolds, zinnias, any bright flowers that will attract her. I coax her onto the sugar-sweet flowers and put her back in the box. I was afraid she'd be easy prey for the birds.

The Painted Lady sits, trying to protect herself with her bent wings up, shivering, trying to warn away predators, a regressive, useless way of defending herself because she has no other. Her wings adhere to the excess sugar, a testament to my overzealous care, and she gets stuck, upside down, pumping her wings wildly, but to no avail. I reach in to free her, leaving a little of her useless wing behind.

In a dream that night, David and I drink through the long, curvy straws that he used in speech therapy to strengthen his mouth muscles. It is a bitter drink, maybe absinthe or tea made from herbs. He gets up and tries to jump to hit some decorations that are hanging from the ceiling for the Fourth of July. I try to pick him up to reach, but he doesn't want my help. He keeps jumping and trying to jump, jumping funny with one of his legs hanging down weak.

My mother comes in. She is Pauline the way I saw her as a small child. I am young, wearing a worn red flannel nightgown that covers my undeveloped legs and the flat feet that Pauline tried to correct through the use of "cookies" in my shoes. She takes my face in her hands and she is crying. "Lisele, Lisele," she says, using my Yiddish name, one she only uses when I am sick. She looks past me, as if I'm already gone, and I feel deeply afraid. Something is wrong, but I don't know what.

When I awake, I am crying.

I know that it is time to let the Painted Lady go, but I still can't.

"It's not much of a life in a box, Mom," Dan chides. He takes the Painted Lady on his finger, bringing her out to the deep blue hydrangea she seemed to favor. He hides her under a leaf and builds a cocoon of hosta leaves to protect her.

When we return from swimming, she is gone. But I look under the leaves the next morning and the morning after that.

## Reading and Writing: End of Third Grade

I still have more trouble with words like *was* or *and* or *the.* Mommy says that is because those words don't make a picture in your mind. I still have to memorize each and every one of those words. I still sometimes mistake "the" for "to." When I write them, sometimes I'll put in "and" for "the." I still mix up b and d. I still sometimes miss those small words or skip a line. I still like to use my finger to point. It's good to read things over, the first time you read it you try and figure out the words. The second time you try and figure out what they are saying.

I'd never go read a storybook unless I have to for school. And I'm always counting how many chapters it has. I try to read the last chapter first because most of the time for a book report you only have to know a little of the story. If you know how it turns out you don't have to read the whole book so carefully. Also, it helps if you know the story beforehand and have heard the words in the book before. Then they are easier to read. If the print in the book is too small, I won't choose it, either. I'd rather do something that's too easy, even if it's not so interesting. I'd much rather play with my G.I. Joes or get information from Discovery Channel. It's easier. It's still work to read. I'll read books if there's really something I want to know about. I still like books with pictures, but I can read a lot more of the information. I like going to the bookstore. I just got a book on Pearl Harbor and one on the history of World War II.

Dan is learning to read now, and when he reads a word I'll think to myself, *That's so easy, anybody could read that.* But I still feel nervous when I look at a big book. I feel like I'm not going to be able to do it, or it will take too long. That's really it. It'll take so long, and I'll never get to do any of the other things I want to do. I don't want to spend all that time. My tutor says that I really can read anything now, but if it's too long, I feel like I won't be able to do it, even if I can. I don't like new things or new places. They make me nervous. I don't like new books, unless it's on something that I already knew about, like war.

Writing, in the beginning, was very hard. I wrote in print, and in first grade, I thought script was like doodles. I was improving in my print near the end of first grade, but it was nowhere near excellent. I made a lot of mistakes in the way I wrote the letters. Like when I was taking a spelling test one day, one of my teachers was helping me, and every two seconds the teacher would correct me. Either there was a letter backwards, or I didn't close one of my a's. And I felt so mad that I couldn't do anything, that I couldn't do it right. I felt so stupid, even though I spelled the words right. When I would print, I couldn't even read my own handwriting because it was so sloppy. I couldn't get my hand to make letters the way I wanted, and they were all over the page because I can't tell how much room I have to the end of the page so then I put in one of those little dash things to continue the word on the next line. Or I would start writing in the middle of the page instead of the red line. Now I fold the paper and start on the fold.

In second grade we started script, but it was hard for me. I could barely do it. I tried to write in print all the time because I was so bad in script. I hated writing in script in the beginning because it was just one more thing I had to learn and I already knew how to print. At the end of second grade, I forgot script and I never wanted to do it again. In third grade I had to learn script all over again because now they made you to write script all the time. I went to a special handwriting class, and Mrs. Harris taught me. Soon it was getting easier, and by the middle of the year it was easy to write in script. Now I always write in script. Script writing is better, and now my script is really neat. It's easier once you get it because you don't have to keep stopping and starting new letters and your hand kind of memorizes some of the words without having to think about it. And there are less backwards letters. It's only the b and the d I still mess up.

I feel kind of stupid whenever I have to write a lot. When I have to write it just takes a while. My hand was . . . it is always just so slow and I skip over words without meaning to. I know what I want to say, but I lose words when I try to write it down. Why is that?

If I make a mistake, I can't usually find the mistake, and by the time I find the mistake, sometimes I've forgotten what I wanted to say. Now the sentence doesn't make sense to me anymore. I get lost where I'm writing. Then I have to look everywhere, and then I have to start writing all over again because I write the wrong words cause I'm already thinking about something else. It's just as bad when I have to copy something over, which I always do because they are always correcting my spelling on my rough drafts, but copying over the correct spellings I still make mistakes. I don't try to write shorter answers, though. Not really. But I see that some of my friends do that. They try to use words that they can spell or not say too much.

I can never stand to go back and try to see the mistakes myself. There are so many rules about how to write sentences. Mommy says, "Just the I, just make that a capital. Just remember one rule," but I still don't. I can remember now, like to start sentences with a capital and to end with a period. But when I am writing, I am in a hurry and it would take too long to do all those things, and I can't remember when I'm doing it. There are too many rules like that for me to remember them all, and I just want to get done. I want to do other things like watch TV or draw or organize my Pokémon cards into different groups.

## Lost in the Forest

The cries of children outside at recess could be mistaken for a revolution in a small South American country. Nervous about the results of David's three-year reevaluation, I am focused on dust moats moving with surprising passion through a square of sunlight on the school psychologist's desk.

"David tested in the ninety-ninth percentile of intellectual functioning, Mrs. Siever."

Momentarily preoccupied with the geometry of color, I barely notice her genuine smile. She's really happy for David. And for me. You don't often get to tell a parent such good news.

*What was that story? "De Maupassant"—"The Necklace." The one where a woman borrows her friend's diamond necklace and loses it. Secretly, she buys a replacement and spends her whole life paying off the debt. At the end, after she's old, ugly, and poor, she confesses her sacrifice. The friend tells her the necklace was paste, a fake.*

Surprised by my lack of response, the psychologist pushes the paper listing the scores across the desk. Staring at them, part of me is ecstatic, selfishly vindicated. *I knew he was smart.* But I can't stop thinking of this story. Could our worry have been for nothing? The narrow tunnel our world has become, me and David, David and me—husband, career, and pleasure jettisoned; his childhood filled with disappointment—all for nothing? The dyslexia will not cripple him. Not in school. But who will give him back those years when he should have been only adored? Who will give Larry and me back that time? A strange draft, elation mixed with bitterness.

My anxiety initiates the switch into "Dr. Weinstein" mode. I review the scores as if they belong to someone else's child in my office. Hm . . . mm. Ver-ry interesting. The results are quite different from Dr. Martin's, reflecting the fact that some of the test items that discriminate average from superior are the very questions young dyslexic children have the most trouble with—days of the week, coin names, the month after February, or things that call for rapid retrieval of names. David's motor skills have also improved with age, so he gets credit for doing some items faster. He's still dyslexic, of course. It's not unusual for dyslexic children to test artificially low because the Weschler IQ tests are so language-based. But it's still a shock to see how much the IQ scores, which I was taught to think of as stable over time, changed once David got remedial help.

*Well, I guess he doesn't need me anymore. He's smart. He'll find his own way. We're out of the woods. I shouldn't do so much for him. No more homework help or typing the book reports.*

When I tell David, the numbers and my reassuring words mean nothing.

"Does that mean I'm smart, Mommy? How can they tell if I'm smart? You're not just saying that? Am I really smart?"

My feeling that he can do it on his own is not shared by David.

Clutching at his throat like a man trying to loosen the noose, David pleads, "Help me, help me Mommy. Why won't you help me anymore?" Digging in his heels, he refuses to work alone, or with anyone but me. He is shocked when his beloved teacher fails him after he refuses to copy over his book report. He gets rude to Mrs. Greene and tells her to go home. The school starts talking about the benefits of a self-enclosed classroom again.

Does he want to fail? He doesn't need me intellectually, but then what is it? He wants to maintain our special relationship, to have me sit quietly beside him as he works. He might be smart, but he doesn't feel independent.

"What would you do if you were lost in the forest in the daytime?" This question from the Weschler IQ test taunts me like a quiz show query. On the IQ test, you look for a rational answer—check the side of the trees the moss grows on, see that the sun always sets in the West, follow a stream. The Yellow Brick Road was clearly marked for reading. We found a good tutor, arranged David's school career, and offered a language-rich environment. But more is needed to get from here to there than remediation. Did poppies make us sleep? We are not out of the woods yet.

## PART VI

# A Horse of a Different Color:
# Dyslexia, Development, and Identity

*"Scientific observation is not merely pure description of separate facts. Its main goal is to view an event from as many perspectives as possible. In the end we must find the 'inner laws' that produce the uniqueness of each event in its setting; we must finally ascend to the concrete."*

—A. R. Luria
The Making of Mind

# Chapter 11

## Perspectives

"Mommy, just give me $10.00 for lunch at the deli."

"David, how could you possibly need $10.00 for lunch? Forget it. How much could a sandwich cost? Are you planning to use the extra money for a toy? No way."

"I really need it. I do. I do. I do. Why don't you believe me? You never believe me."

Violating every boundary of personal space, David assumes his argument's power is directly proportional to how physically close he can get to me. I retreat to the bathroom. *He couldn't need a toy that badly. Does he owe a friend money? Is a bully taking advantage of him?*

Shouting through the locked door: "I don't need it for lunch. I need it so I don't have to give them the right amount of money at the lunch counter. I'm not good with money. I'm never sure. What if I count wrong? Or forget that the nickel is five cents and not twenty-five? That's why I need $10.00. If I give them $10.00, I couldn't possibly have ordered more than $10.00 worth of food. They'll give me the right change. No one will know."

*How little I see of his trials.*

"Here David. Here's $10.00 in one-dollar bills. Give them one dollar more than they ask for. That'll solve the problem."

\*     \*     \*

The school nurse tells David that he had trouble reading the eye chart and might need glasses. He calls me, sobbing. "Please don't tell Daddy. Don't tell your friends. They can't make me get them, can they?"

"What's the big deal? I wear glasses."

"Everything has to be fixed with me."

Terrified that one more thing could be wrong, especially something that can be seen, David watches others carefully. In the morning, his clothing must be exactly right, just like the other kids'. His hair, just so. Originality is a luxury for the securely normal.

As adults we arrange our lives to skirt humiliation. Avoiding what we don't do well, we calm ourselves with memories of success. David has no lifetime of triumphant images to soothe him when the going is rough. For him, there's no way out. School is his job; he has to go. He has to read out loud if the teacher says to, even when the letters make no sense to him. He has to go to gym and play soccer even when he's not sure what direction the goal is or how to get there at the same time as the ball. He has to worry that the kids will tease him because he can only do two sit-ups when they do forty. He has to try to tie his shoes even if his fingers don't have the dexterity to make little rabbit ears. Otherwise, he could go to the principal for not listening. Every new day brings potential mortification, the imminent sense of danger slowly eroding his pride.

How much energy it takes to be him—just to do things that most of us do unconsciously—just to maintain his balance.

*Being learning disabled is a full-time job.*


## Developmental Perspectives

Could our nightly melodrama over the homework be normal? Decoding written language might be a finite process, but dyslexia is turning out to be a far more complicated dilemma than attaching sounds to written symbols.

After ten years of postdoctoral psychoanalytic training, infant research, associate director of the Parent Infant Center at the New York

Psychoanalytic Institute, and professor of psychology you'd think I understood something about mothers and children. But the *Sturm und Drang* of my endlessly entangled relationship with David was not the smooth developmental trajectory I had been taught in graduate school. Confused, I consult Leon Hoffman, director of the Pacella Parent Child Center and the father of an older learning disabled child.

"Lissa, don't you know? I still read my daughter's books with her. And she's off in college. Doing fantastically, by the way. We're reading novels about Asian women." Leon absentmindedly rubs his stomach, looking for a moment like a preoccupied expectant female. His glorious identification with his daughter helps a thought coalesce. Maybe learning disabled children don't separate from their parents as quickly as their peers. Maybe we shouldn't expect them to.

"So Leon, what else is different for these kids besides reading?"

"Lissa, analysts haven't really applied their understanding of child development to this area. The best way I can say it is—for the mother, it's sort of the same and sort of different as regular motherhood. A bit more intense all around for everyone."

*So much for the oral tradition.*

I head back to the library, hoping for help with these psychological "side effects," which are now seeming worse than the illness itself. I find papers on the unconscious wishes and family constellations of dyslexic children written by psychoanalysts in the forties; all ignore the neurological roots of reading problems. One paper claims reading problems are due to "oral sadistic" conflicts because the letters unconsciously represent real objects that are being devoured. Another blames dyslexia on maternal tendencies to infantalize the child, leaving him unable to acquire the necessary skills. *I really loved that one.* One maddening paper attributes causality to the meaning of dyslexic reading errors, claiming, for example, that reading "was" for "saw" involves a wish to confuse past and present. The papers seem bizarre, very cart-before-the-horse, disregarding the possibility that having cognitive problems will cause psychological conflicts or exacerbate existing ones.

The papers by cognitive neuroscientists were equally one-sided, offering their impersonal neurological model. Once the biological basis of dyslexia was identified, scholars ignored how it was experienced, as well as its human toll—the effects on the child's development and the social fabric of his life. Instead, papers proliferated on anatomical focus, genetic roots, and the specifics of the reading process. The scientists and the analysts never talked to each other, never attempted to close the gap between physical and mental. Both approaches seem relevant but also incomplete.

The more I read, the more I start to feel like a cut-out Betsy McCall doll, half-dressed in one paper outfit, half in another: scientist/analyst. Not to mention mother. I have a *real* child, not a collection of abstract postulates. If I could account for his genetic heritage by describing the four pairs of neucleotides arranged in triplets, would that tell me who David was? David has dyslexia, but his complicated development is more than just an epiphenomenon of brain morphology. Dyslexia influences how David feels about himself, how he interacts with others, how he manages his anger, and how he chooses his interests. But it's not the only ingredient in the mix. His temperament, Larry and my reactions, and the calamities that shape all children's lives are also factors—anxieties about separation, the fear of loss of love, concerns about the integrity of the body, and guilt over real and imagined transgressions. Still, the question remains: How can a processing problem, one that can be compensated for through a combination of creativity, technology, and remediation, become so pivotal to the child's identity?

The simple answer: It's a different mind. The brain bears a special relationship to identity, to what we define as self. We would have no trouble believing that we were still ourselves even after something as radical as a heart transplant, but we understand that a brain transplant would make us someone else. Further, the same alterations in a dyslexic child's brain function that cause trouble with academic skills are present long before school starts. They affect every phase of the child's psychological development. Factors such as the ability to bond, regulate physical states, handle emotions, and acquire the motoric and psychological skills that support a smooth exodus from the protective orbit of the mother-child relationship are altered for the learning disabled child.

One small example: From birth, dyslexic children have more trouble discriminating phonemes. They are infants who can't easily tell "ba" from "ka." It is on the patterning of these sounds that differential meanings are assigned. If the sound pattern is not stable, then associating a stable meaning to the sound becomes difficult. A lot of variance in the signal makes it harder for the child to understand what's normal, and the world becomes a much more confusing and anxiety-producing place. If words don't have stable meanings, neither will a parent's directions or prohibitions. What substitutes for word meaning? Feeling— our primitive way of knowing the world. In an emotional moment, can the child trust what the words say? The possibility for misunderstanding is everywhere. All this goes on long before the child reads. If the child's wiring is generating a lot of "noise," then the invariant patterns that are the fabric of our relation to reality will be harder to discern. A lot more repetition will be necessary to provide a feeling of safety and predictabilitry. It then becomes incumbent upon the parents to provide that structure. The child's neurocognitive problems as well as the increased stress put on the mother-child relationship make it harder for learning disabled children to form coherent narratives about themselves—to develop an acceptable picture of who they are in the world that will support a stable self-esteem.

"David, what's yellow?"

"What do you mean, Mom?"

"Like, is mustard yellow? Is the sun yellow?"

"No, they are different, completely different. Mustard is *mustard* yellow. And the sun is *sun* yellow. But if you want, I could put some mustard on a plate and go out in the sun and compare them."

Apart from the recognition that David is a true empiricist, the interchange is informative. For me, yellow is yellow. I never think about yellow because I have the word *yellow*. Yellow is yellow, and so is mustard, and so is the sun. But David has no color name. Inherently categories, names are how we organize the world, allowing us to group varied experiences together, saving us the effort of having to perceive the world anew every day. He might be using the same rods and cones to identify yellow that I do, but lacking quick access to the color category yellow, David's *experience* of yellow is far more differentiated. And precise.

I'm working with an 8 Crayola Crayon Box and he's got a 500

Crayola Crayon Box. (Incidentally, this turns out to be true in the auditory realm as well. Dyslexic children turned out to be unable to categorize tones, because they were more sensitive to the interstitial tones than nondyslexic children.) Sounds great? Who wouldn't want a 500 box? What writer wouldn't kill for a 500 Crayon Box?

The problem presents itself in a new light when Larry and I decide to paint the living room red. Everyone knows red. Fire engine red. Santa and the elves. Stop signs. A trip to the hardware store proves me wrong. Old-Fashioned Milk Paint offers Barn Red and Salem Red. Moving on to Pittsburgh Paints Historic Colors, I find Cedar Chest, Baked Bean, and Amaretto (which seems too brown). Now I'm developing an eye. Maybe I want a red that is really more blue. I try Glidden paints and find Deep Garnet, Scarlett's Velvet, Burgundy, Cranberry Zing, and Cerise. None of these seem right, but I'm not sure. On to Benjamin Moore Custom Colors. Ralph Lauren offers Congo Red and Bookbinder Red. Tempted by the opportunity to deal with the now simpler-seeming world of meaning rather than perception, I tell myself, *Well you are writing a book*. But it's only a false hope. Bookbinder red isn't a magical tie to publication. It's just some girl in an office naming paint colors. Anyway, it's too dark . . . Who could imagine so many reds?

I end up at Janovic Plaza, where the colors are given numbers but no names, classified like the Dewey decimal system, breaking down into smaller and smaller intervals, dangerously proliferating shades. I grab swatches by the dozens and paste them on the walls in the living room to check the effects of light. I can't leave the house without seeing red. Red is everywhere! On my chopsticks, my lipstick, my laquer stools, my pocketbook, the red pen I correct student papers with, a jacket bought in a fit of daring. Paralyzed with indecision, mad with the burden of choice.

I'm passionate for red, fired up, burnt out. I can't think of anything else. Finally, a solution emerges—linen white. Sometimes, it's better not to look too closely.

Hermann Rorschach, originator of the famous inkblots, suggested that how much a person's color perception dominated their experience of an ambiguous inkblot was correlated with how they dealt with feelings. Everyday language supports his insight. We use colors to describe emotion—green with envy, blue for sadness, red for passion or anger. Maybe David's difficulty naming colors is one aspect of a larger problem mediating the sensory world through language. What if it partakes of the same process as naming emotions? Or being able to sort out the nuances of feeling without being inundated?

David can't easily and quickly access a simple word that allows him to wall off experience. I watch David's rubbery face as he imitates others, picking up subtle nuances in gesture that I don't see until he mimics them. His extraordinary receptiveness to animals also suggests a multisensory way of engaging the world. It's face to face, muscle to muscle, percept to percept—an imitative way of knowing. Language doesn't screen out things for him, certainly not in the heat of the situation. Each emotional situation must be experienced afresh and assessed, not just simply put in a box with words, like "Daddy is mad but not so mad—just leave me alone for a few minutes mad." No wonder he's always in my face, when I need a "time-out" to calm down. He has to figure it out every time. It's a world of images and sensations, not easily checked against memories. Language is also necessary for coding temporal states—you need it to tell yourself that you will not always feel this way, or that Mommy will be back soon even if you miss her. David's visceral way of understanding is probably a richer experience, a benefit in the right setting. After all, he's *seeing* red and I'm not, really. But it's also a liability, leaving him more anxious and uncertain, needing a parent to mediate and filter his experience.

## The Mother Child Matrix

Where is that "good enough" mother anyway? Popular culture offers a picture of the ordinary devoted mother who, although not perfect, provides a sufficiently secure base from which her child can grow and develop. This concept, taken from D. W. Winnicott, a British psychoanalyst, was a progressive one in an era when mothers were blamed for everything from schizophrenia to psychopathy. Yet few academic or popular writings speak to the reality of motherhood, a nearly impossible profession rife with contradictions. Powerful and helpless, at one moment a mother "bestrides the Earth like a Colossus;" one second later she is impotent before the whims of a small tyrant. Every new mother swears she will be different from her mother. But caring for her baby immerses her in intense memories of her own mother, reconnecting them at a time when she is trying desperately to separate and define her own maternal identity. What work besides motherhood is so full of exquisite highs and despairing lows; what other work so sorely strains one's previously adequate abilities to maintain self-control and to tolerate loving and hating the same person? Although mothers are allowed to have needs for nurturance, the experience of intense sadness or anger on the mother's part are seen as less acceptable, even though every mother knows they are inevitable.

Despite the magnitude of the task, and the volatile emotions it generates, one of mother's most important roles is to mediate her child's feeling states, so that they don't become too overwhelming or disorganizing. How does she do this? In what can look like an elegant synchronous dance, a mother senses her child's emotions, feels in her body their shape and texture, and mirrors them back to her child using her voice and facial expressions. She calms and reassures the child, intensifying pleasurable states and modifying his distress. Through this process, the child becomes aware of her as a predictable "other"; through the reflection she provides, he will come to recognize himself and his feelings, forming a nascent sense of identity. Eventually he will realize that others are like him, with a mind like his own. Developmental psychologists use the term containment for this process, but it is much more active than being a vessel. A mother must let herself experience her child's distress (or extreme pleasure), then allow herself to become consciously aware of her own reactions so that she doesn't overamplify his feelings. The aim is to keep them in a range tolerable for the child. To do this, she has to be able to shift between identifying with her child and staying firmly rooted in her identity as a mother. It's tricky, even with the most steady, easygoing child.

The job of containment is far more difficult when the child has a learning disability. One set of potential problems are internal to the child. Cognitive differences such as exceptional abilities, special sensitivities, or developmental delays affect the child's temperament and vulnerabilities, often making it harder for the mother to read the child's emotional states or know what will be soothing for him. In addition, processing problems make it more difficult for the child to form a unified picture of the parent that is stable and predictable.

A second set of difficulties grows out of a mother's reactions to her child's problems. When each of us was young, we wished, like all children, to be perfect and all-powerful; perhaps for a moment we were, made strong by our mother's infatuated look that reached beyond her body to hold us. Eventually, the world intruded and sadly we realized we didn't make the flowers grow. We weren't Peter Pan or Snow White, or probably even the prettiest girl in the fifth grade. This wish for a flawless self goes underground, but it has strong roots and waits for a new spring to grow. That time often arrives when a woman is pregnant, her changing body reviving a long forgotten dream. "Surely," she tells herself, "this child, my child, will be the child of magic perfection." No flesh-and-blood child can match this ideal, and every real child inevitably disappoints. Luckily, the process of coming to see each other as separate beings with their own individual reality and needs is a lengthy journey and mother and child have time to adapt. Usually, this fall from grace doesn't cause more pain than we can bear.

In contrast, the mother of a child with problems has to give up her fantasy of the perfect child at a time when that child is still experienced as part of her body and when the child's imagined perfection is part of her self-image. A mother who is unable to bear her child's imperfection will have a harder time empathizing or taking care of his needs. The child's difficulties might make the mother feel that she is damaged or that her body has been hurtful. Who would want to be around something that makes you feel so bad? Her anger at her child for making her feel this way and subsequent guilt may lead to withdrawal, or to seeking refuge in an identification with the more critical aspects of her own mother. Paradoxically, the child who needs the most consistent involvement may get the least.

At some point, every parent dislikes or even feels hatred toward his or her own child. Awareness of such feelings is always disturbing. Normally, we feel absolved because our children keep growing "despite" us, despite what we imagine we have done to them. Over time, we learn to say "No" and to bear their anger toward us. But a child's continual failure makes it harder for a mother to really believe that her anger hasn't caused harm, or to feel "good enough." She may try, ever harder, to give him everything and forgo her own needs. Thus guilt over anger can also lead to an overinvolved mother who believes she must sacrifice everything for her child. Neither solution is adaptive.

Why are relationships with parents, and later parental substitutes like teachers, so crucial to the success of learning disabled children? All children use their attachments to adults to regulate tension and keep themselves from feeling flooded by painful emotions or just too much stimulation. Learning disabled children need to rely even more on adults for scaffolding. Their ability to generate their own self-controlling structures is more limited, and their cognitive problems make it harder for them to experience the world as a predictable, regular place. Forming stable internal models of people's behavior and expectations of them requires more repetition than it does for other children.

Further, learning disabled children live in a world they are more likely to experience as overwhelming and fearful. The printed word itself becomes associated with continued failure; it can then act as an aversive stimulus that spurs avoidance. (Think Pavlov and rats jumping out of cages to avoid shock.) This behavioral avoidance then makes it impossible for the decoding process to become automatic. Strong attachments mediate fear, in humans just as much as rat pups, who show less fear in novel situations if they're handled and groomed a lot as infants. Although no one would suggest licking your learning disabled child (a favorite behavior of rat pup mothers), a hug and the continued reassurance of the parent's love may lessen the terror of opening a new door. Curiosity grows out of the affective matrix of the early mother-child interaction and continues to need the social world to support it. If the context of the parent-child relationship acts to allay fear by providing pleasure or nurturance in learning, the child is less likely to avoid new tasks.

The clock, set five minutes ahead to fool us into getting to the bus stop on time, reads 7:10. David is still not awake.

7:20. He's up, dressed, and downstairs. The bus is at 7:51.

*All right. No fight this morning. Pauline, you drill sergeant, you can be proud of me now. I'll make it to the staff meeting at the Parent Infant Center on time for once.*

7:41. David starts looking for his math homework.

*Pride goes before a fall.*

"Someone lost it. When you cleaned the kitchen last night, Mom, you threw it out."

"No, I didn't see it."

"Yes, you did. You did. I can't find it."

Miraculously, the math homework is retrieved under some of Dan's drawings. *Are we out of the woods?*

"I forgot to write a few sentences on my Australia report. On the weather. Could you write them for me?"

"David, I have to get to work. Write them yourself." *Not so fast, Pauline.*

7:47. David starts to write. The bus is a far-gone hope. He'll have to be driven to school. I'll never make it to Manhattan by 9:30.

"I have to leave, David. Dad will take you."

"You can't leave, Lissa. You can't. I haven't finished yet. Dad isn't even up. I'll be late for school. I'll need a late pass. Please, Lissa."

*I know he's developed that voice to drive me crazy.* Rather than listen to the whining, I give in. *You wimp, Lissa. You always give in.*

8:20. In the car, doors slammed.

8:25. Careening around a curb, I rip my tire.

"There's a strange sound coming from the car, Mom."

We pull over by the reservoir. Flat. I'm going to miss my meeting waiting for the tow truck. My cell phone, purchased for emergencies, is out of batteries. Turning around, I scream, "I hate you, David. I hate you when these things happen. Can't we just for one morning pretend we are normal?"

We sit silently, knowing I have crossed some line, both stunned by the immediacy of the human heart's ability to make pain.

"Mom, it's not my fault you ripped your tire. You can't go and blame everything on me. If you resent taking me, you should just say 'no' . . . I hate my life."

A neighbor comes by and graciously offers to take David to school.

David, usually quite reticent with strangers, jumps eagerly into her car while I await the goodness of Triple AAA.

That evening, David chooses *Rotten Island,* William Steig's brilliant children's story about a "very unbeautiful, very rocky rotten island," for his bedtime book. The island is inhabited by hideously ugly creatures who "loved hating and hissing at one another, taking revenge, tearing and breaking things, screaming, roaring, caterwauling, venting their hideous feeling. It tickled them to be cruel and to give each other bad dreams . . . Nothing could make these monsters shake so hard with laughter as to see another one suffering pain." Tonight, I recognize myself as an island creature, my morning performance like a cat snarling in an alley. The book reminds us that cruelty and anger are a part of life, and even at times, a part of pleasure.

"Why did you get in the car with someone you didn't know, David?"

"I figured I was safer with a stranger than with you."

## Steps Toward Individuation and Internalization

Becoming a truly separate individual is a long haul, a lengthy afterbirth hatching that develops along with the child's maturing cognitive capacities. It's not surprising that crucial aspects of attachment and individuation are altered in children with processing difficulties. For example, the child who has problems sorting out visual information might not develop a specific tie to his mother as quickly, or the bond might depend on other forms of sensory input such as sounds that are easier for the child to process. After a specific attachment forms, it might also be harder for the child to separate.

Normally, at about one year old, along with the development of independent walking, children have a "love affair with the world." Not yet aware of their vulnerable state, the child acts as though he is invincible. Fear develops along with the child's awareness of how small he is in relation to a large and unpredictable world, usually around eighteen months. This recognition is a blow to all children; negotiating the ensuing crisis is much more complicated for children with processing problems. For example, a child with a speech and language delay can't ask for what he wants. Gestures, less specific and more subject to misinterpretation, lead to frustration. The increased tantrum behavior makes both mother and child feel awful. Similarly, a child with a weak visual memory might need a closer connection to his mother because it is harder to hold on to her image when she is gone. The child's difficulty separating at age-appropriate times such as nursery school then contributes to the parent's feeling of failure, which further compromises her ability to empathize with the child's dilemma. The processing problems and the parent's feelings of inadequacy become a vicious circle.

The natural push of childhood is toward independence. Unless a child feels unable to cope, he will take over functions that were originally performed by his parents. Learning disabled youngsters need their parents more—to help them learn, to control their impulses, and to mediate a world they experience as difficult. The parent, of necessity, begins to function as an auxiliary ego for the child, filling in for what the child can't do himself. For learning disabled children, needs become drawn into conflicts, and it is often impossible to differentiate need and demand. A child might ask for help after it is no longer necessary, because getting help has taken on other psychological meanings, such as being a sign of the parent's love. Similarly, the child might be unable to overcome his anxiety about trying a task he could realistically master. Thus, individuation takes a lot longer. The normal desire to possess the parent for one's own usually peaks in the five- to seven-year period, at the same time as the discovery of the reading problems. The necessity of greater-than-ordinary parental involvement in the child's life makes it harder to resolve the usual incestuous fantasies of childhood. They can't just tell the parent to "go away."

And if the parents are saints? Godlike in their ability to manage the child's anguish and assuage his fears? Would there still be problems? Unfortunately, yes. The coexistance between an important psychological development and the usual time of discovery of the learning problems (if not by the school, than through the child's own awareness of difference) makes the disability a continuing influence on the child's personality. A very young child's sense of who and how worthwhile they are *is* what they see reflected in the eyes of their parents. Although this puts a greater burden on the mother, these early self-images tend to be mutable and short-lived, making it easier to protect and soothe the child. When they are young, a kiss really does take away pain, and Mommy's belief in their perfection can forestall any doubts to the contrary.

As a child reaches the age of seven, give or take a year, he begins to develop a more stable self-image that he carries around "inside him." Because this new internalized image is more autonomous from how the child is responded to by significant others, it helps the child separate from his parents. It is also harder to change by altering external circumstances. The picture a child carries around of himself now becomes a determining factor in how the world will subsequently be experienced, as the child "organizes" new experience in concordance with his self-image. Any awareness on the child's part of a cognitive problem is stored in memory along with other senses of deficiency such as concerns about gender identity, feelings about his body, and worries about how lovable he is. Triggering one worry will make it more likely that the others come to consciousness as well. Put together, they give a negative taint to the self-picture.

Add to this already volatile situation the fact that children live in the tyranny of the present tense. For them, it will always be "this way." They don't have the perspective of the future or the solace of history. They don't know that other kids with their same problem turned out okay. To have something wrong, something you don't even have a name for, is a never-ending torture.

The "facts" of the learning disability are less powerful determinants of the final psychological outcome than the meaning of the cognitive problems to the child, the way in which the child's fantasies interact with the other developmental crises of childhood, and the ability of the parents to nurture and protect the child's self-esteem.


"Doll, you and the boys can sit over there."

The harried waitress, order pad poised midway between apron pocket and pencil, indicates two seats together at the counter and a third separated by a pass-through. She recognizes Dave and Dan. Trying to be kind, she bumps them ahead of the other cold crushed suburbanites who will be waiting a half hour for Sunday breakfast at

Bella's. David and Dan stand frozen-footed from the unavoidable slush they have met grousing their way up the hill, hair still wet from swim class. We love this dark stucco cave of a luncheonette with its Dutch blue naugahyde booths, decadent homemade donuts, and double-fried French toast. Anyone who can still call me "doll" gets my cooperation.

"Dave, you sit over there, across. I'll sit here with Danny."

"No, no," his voice starting the half-tone escalation to whine. "Let Dan sit there. Dan, that's okay with you, right?"

I catch a brief glance of raw fear peeking behind his manipulation as he starts on Dan. His wide-eyed look stops me from insisting. Dan, used to adjusting to David's needs, is already heading dutifully, if unhappily, toward the isolated stool.

"See. It's okay with Dan."

Exasperated, I say, "Fine. We'll all wait." The seats go to a grateful older couple. Later, soothed by cinnamon circles and coffee, egg yolk dripping from the corners of my mouth, I am calm enough to explore.

"David, why couldn't you sit across from us?"

"There was a man there. I didn't know what to make of him. I wanted to be near you, to sit with you. It makes me feel safe."

"But Dave, we could still see you and talk."

"What if I was sitting alone and the waitress didn't know I was with you? What if she tried to talk to me and she couldn't understand what I said? I'd have to say it over and over. Everyone would look at me. What if I wanted French toast and the word *pancakes* came out of my mouth instead? Remember last week with the deli? I said I wanted lox and I meant ham. You said there was no good lox in Irvington, and I kept insisting, and you went to the Tarrytown Gourmet store for lox. I wanted ham. You made me eat it anyway."

My anger deflates. What a fearful world it is for him. Every staircase is potentially malevolent; every street has a curb to trip over. Better to hide in your mind—creating cities and invincible dinosaurs.

## Homework

I am much better now, but in the second and most of the third grade, doing homework was really bad. Mommy and

I had a fight every night. *Every night.* I would always try to put off doing my homework. No matter how hard I worked on it, I knew there was going to be a mistake. Like in the spelling. Or the way I wrote a word.

There'll always be a mistake, no matter how hard I try, so why would I want to start? Mommy would say if I would just start earlier we would have time to make sure it's right instead of waiting till it's almost time to go to bed. Then I feel scared that my teacher will yell at me if I don't get all the homework done and she won't think that I am a good student.

So if it is very late at night, I start whining, "Please, please help me. Please help me," which drives Mommy crazy. But trying to do it early, before I really have to, only makes sense to her. I feel I will always have enough time to do it because I tell myself it's not so hard. I'll have time. I put it off as long as I can. Then Mom yells at me. She says she won't work with me anymore or that I'm not trying, or even worse things than that, like that if I can't do the homework than maybe I should go to a school for kids with reading and writing problems. But I wouldn't know anyone there.

I know Mommy will always stay up with me and help me finish. But she'll be mad at me. Then I'll feel hurt and alone inside and have to hope that tomorrow we won't be mad at each other. I always say before we go to sleep, "Are we friends? Can we just forget it and be friends?" If we are not friends, I worry that I will have bad dreams. Usually we do make up. But then when I come home from school, it's going to start again. But it is really better this year. We used to fight every night. But now, there's a lot of the homework I can do. I'm learning my multiplication facts. I got a sheet from my teacher congratulating me, and we hung it on the refrigerator. Last year I couldn't even remember 2 × 2. So I can do my math homework by myself without any help.

Mommy won't always correct my homework carefully. After I've done it, I just want to leave it to her to take care of and to correct the spelling and the punctuation. If I had to copy it over again, I would never do it. Never! Because it takes me a really long time to write, and if I'm copying I make even more mistakes sometimes than when I am trying to sound a word out. Mommy said, "Can't we spell the word *they* the same way twice in one paragraph?" She doesn't get it. Each time I try to sound it out, it sounds a little different. Sometimes it sounds like "t-h-a-y" or "t-h-i-y" and sometimes "t-h-e-y."

Sometimes, Mommy is in a rush or she wants me to try to do it myself. She doesn't correct it perfectly and then I feel like she thinks I'm hopeless. I feel mad at her that she is a crummy mother. I want her to feel bad, too. When we had pizza lunch at school, I told Mommy that the mothers from the Parent Teacher's Association had made the pizza themselves. I said, "They are not like you. They would do anything for their children." Mommy laughed that time. When she isn't careful, I think it doesn't matter to her how I do in school because I'll never do well. Okay, I'm an idiot. She should correct it better. You see, it's okay to make mistakes with your mother, but it is really terrible to be embarrassed in front of your teachers. I never do homework with Dad, either. Dad is really smart. Or the other kids could get to see your grade, and it's "Needs Improvement," NI. I hate to see that NI.

It's really important to me that Mom takes it seriously. I really like her to be there next to me when I do it, because every time it gets hard I stop working. Even sometimes when I can do it myself I really need her to do it with me anyway, because I never totally feel sure that I can do it. Then Mommy says, "See, you could do it. You didn't need me." But I did. Maybe not to do it with me. I don't know. Sometimes, I get mad and I say that I don't care about things like how I do on a book report. But I always do. I just get afraid that I can't do good.

Some things help. It helps if I have something else I

want to do. Like if it's a night where I can see my favorite TV program if I have all my homework done, then I might try to do it quickly as soon as I come home. Otherwise I say, "Oh, that homework is so easy." I tell myself and I really believe it won't take me any time at all. No one can tell me different. No matter how many times I've done the same homework and it took me a long time. I'm sure I have plenty of time to waste, and I can watch an hour or two of TV. Then it's time for dinner. All of a sudden it is late. It's time for bath and I still have my reading homework, my spelling homework, the sentences that I hate the most, and my ABC order (alphabetizing). Thursdays are the worst, because I also have a spelling test to study for.

I don't mind making mistakes, like in reading, because I know I'm not exactly the best at that. I'm used to making mistakes when I read, but I hate like if I make mistakes in ABC order. I try to do it really quick because I don't like it, but if the words are hard or if there are a lot of words starting with the same letter, then I make mistakes. Or sometimes, I just put the words that start with N before the words that start with F. I don't know why. Or if I do a scrap copy and try to copy over my own writing, then I might copy it wrong or spell the spelling words incorrectly and end up having to do the whole thing over during recess. And doing a scrap copy is just too much writing. It's hard for me to go up and down all the word list looking for the A's then the B's. I miss some of the words. It's easier if I have the alphabet in front of me, but I still might skip my eye over them. If I have to do it over, I start to feel stupid, like anybody should be able to alphabetize, but I can't always do it. I always leave one word out. In third grade, they would let you stick that extra word in next to the word before it, but I hear in fourth grade they don't let you do that. You have to write the whole list over. I try to get Mommy to write it over for me. Mommy also copies over the vocabulary words for me, because it is too much writing on these little lines on the index cards that we write the vocabulary words on. I don't have any trouble learning the vocabulary words. I like that part. But it takes me so long to copy the definitions, and I always copy it wrong so then I get messed up that way. Mommy said she would talk to my teacher so maybe I wouldn't have to write them because I don't learn from copying over anyway. Mommy says I'd be better on the computer, but I don't like to type, either. I press the keys too hard and it comes out like DDDDDDDDD when I am writing my name.

## Personality Constellations

At the American Academy of Child and Adolescent Psychiatry meetings, I am on a panel with Jules Glenn. His book, written with Arden Rothstein, on the psychoanalytic treatment of children with learning disabilities is, by far, the most detailed look at the emotional consequences of learning disabilities.

"Dr. Glenn," I tell him, "I loved your book. It really helped me understand things that went on between me and David, especially what you said about how they try to get you angry at them, so when you punish them they can feel like victims. How many times have we been through that one? But the mothers who really need this to know this stuff won't get to read it. Only the professionals will ever see it."

Dr. Glenn, always gracious, offers to let me summarize his conclusions.

Much of what seems like symptomatic behavior or the child's "character" are adaptations to their neurocognitive equipment. Each learning disabled child is different, and the sequela of any deficit will also be influenced by their other intact abilities. Although the specific outcomes are as varied and individual as the types of impairments, some commonalities exist in the psychological picture.

• **Psychological conflict is experienced more intensely.** Daily repeated traumas of frustration and failure lay the groundwork for more profound reactions of sadness when other bad things happen. (They feel intensely sad when something bad happens.)

• **Biological factors make their emotional experiences more intense.** For example, if a child has difficulty taking in, recalling, or categorizing information through words, there will be attempts to compensate by relying on visual information processed through the right hemisphere. This "perceptual hypersensitivity" might leave the child feeling overwhelmed by stimuli. The difficulty differentiating among perceptual stimuli, which are subject to a multitude of interpretations, might heighten anxiety. (They have trouble sorting out what is going on around them.)

• **Because it is harder to put their worries into words, feelings are more likely to get expressed in action.** Their language doesn't always mediate successfully against the direct experience of emotion, because their capacity to form sensible narratives might be compromised by problems in sequence, difficulty with the syntax of language, or an inability to come up with the precise words. (Without the power of words, they often react physically.)

• **Learning disabled children may have more reasons to feel angry, and it is harder for them to find ways to cope with anger.** Typically, children "run" off anger physically, through participation in sports. If problems planning motor activity or difficulties with eye-hand coordination make successful competition impossible, an arena for mastering aggression is lost as well as a source of potential self-esteem. (They often experience a buildup of aggression or anger.)

• **It's more difficult for them to access learning as a way to manage aggression or to find other, acceptable, sublimations.** Acquiring knowledge makes a big world small and manageable. Like any cognitive advance, reading and writing binds emotion by giving it an acceptable form. Children who can't read still need ways to express their feelings. Some find an outlet in drawing, but drawings can't contain the increasing complexity of the narrative structure of the child's fantasy life, and their growing awareness of the skill necessary to make a "good" drawing limits its potential for sublimation, except in cases of rare talent. Drawing as a mode of expression isn't as valued in society as the more standard school-based skills. (They are limited in how they can express emotions as well as creativity.)

• **Children with learning disabilities feel defective.** Often they express concern that their brain is damaged, or that they lack a brain. Because mind is experienced as part of the body, any difficulty learning might also affect feelings about their physicality. Anxiety might show up as a fear of sports, excessive worry about physical damage, a need to borrow the power of others, or a concern about the genitals. (They often become overly concerned with their bodies.)

• **Learning disabled children have more trouble achieving self-directing standards of behavior and conscience.** Often, they identify with the high standards set by their parents and schools. The sense of defect caused by their failure to meet these standards gives rise to a desire to cheat. This is rationalized by their feeling that they have been gypped by having a learning disability. These children are guilty cheaters; carrying out wishes to succeed through cheating, they often invite punishment. (They often break rules, sometimes unintentionally.)

• **Struggles with parents are intense and frequent.** Inevitable battles over schoolwork are magnified by the parent's necessary ongoing involvement. Dyslexic children are angry with parents and teachers, who they blame for not recognizing or preventing their difficulties. They also fear their parents won't love them if they disclose their flaws. (They fight, argue, and act out.)

## Defense

So what does a child do with the painful feelings evoked by having a learning problem? People's ways of warding off emotional pain are as personal as signatures. Some run miles to nowhere in the gym; some become so powerful they never become aware of how weak and frightened they feel; some find ways to suffer, so they don't have to know they are angry. Learning disabled children tend to use more extreme and less adaptive methods of warding off anxiety and sad feelings. They often make use of their cognitive problems in order to avoid becoming upset.

• Denial, a defense supported by their poor or distorted perceptual abilities, as well as their phenomenological experience of "not being able to see," is common. Their parents, wanting to avoid their own experience of narcissistic injury and anger at the child that the learning disabled diagnosis brought to the surface, also use denial. Children identify with their parents' defensive style. What starts out as a denial of the learning problems often generalizes into a way of warding off all emotional upsets.

• Learning disabled children focus on areas where they are superior to others to avoid being aware of what they have trouble with.

• The neuropsychological disabilities are drawn upon to avoid other worries. For example, failing at school might be used to avoid fantasized punishments for outdoing a sibling or parent; being "troubled" might allow a child to maintain an exclusive relationship to a parent.

• They often develop a veneer of "not caring" to avoid disappointment or engage in a grandiose denial of their need to work harder.

• Because of the fewer outlets available for sublimation, they find it harder to shift raw expressions of sexual curiosity or anger into more disguised forms. They are forced to try and get rid of angry or sexual feelings in other ways. They might do something wrong in full sight of their parents because being victimized and yelled at helps them remain unaware of the origin of their anger. Punishment becomes gratifying. These sadomasochistic patterns are extremely confusing and frightening for parents and can lead to a withdrawal from a desperately needy child or a misidentification of the child as "bad."

• Learning disabled children tend to externalize their feelings. They might try to act cruel to others they perceived as victims, as if to say, "It is not me who is the sad and stupid child. It is that child over there. I'm fine." The child might also try to evoke rage and frustration in others in order to exorcize the feeling in themselves.

## Eugenics/Famous Dyslexics

Glass doors push into an eerie, disorienting darkness. Dramatically colored projections on the screens offer the only light at the *Human Genome* exhibit at the Museum of Natural History. A model of a fly's DNA invites us to turn different neon bars on the nucleotide pairs. *Flash!* You've caused a genetic mutation. Other bars have no effect. Talking heads, some of whom are Larry's professional colleagues, project out from the walls, discussing the ethics of a science that holds out the future promise of being able to choose your child's sex, eye color, hair texture, and intelligence.

Dan grabs my coat sleeve tightly. "It's a little creepy in here."

"Oh, just dark, really. What's scaring you?"

"Would you like to do that Mommy? Change how we look, me and David? Did you want us to be different?"

*Do all children worry they are not the ones their parent's wanted?*

At home, I can't push the genetics question out of my mind. Dyslexia has a genetic loading. Is dyslexia one of the things modern gene therapy would select out? Sterilize people with the gene in an effort to control evolutionary destiny? I turn on the computer and type *eugenics* and *dyslexia* into a search engine. There are a horrifying number of sites where the two words exist together. My son, my David, his difficult originality screened out, an accident of DNA, sterilized?

I try another approach, typing in *dyslexic* and *celebrity*. A gold mine of sites offering lists, pictures, and histories from "famous dyslexics." Some I've heard of before: Einstein, Nelson Rockefeller, Werner Von Braun, Thomas Alva Edison. A high concentration of writers: Agatha Christie, William Butler Yeats, John Lennon, Richard Ford, Gustave Flaubert. Artists, visual geniuses like George Balanchine, Leonardo da Vinci, Pablo Picasso, Rennie Mackintosh, the Scottish architect (*we have his chairs in our dining room!*) Robert Raushenberg. Moviemakers and actors like Steven Spielberg, Harrison Ford, Tom Cruise, Henry Winkler, Walt Disney. Serious achievers, people with their own ideas.

Several sites refer to the "gift" of *dyslexia* because of the creative achievements of some dyslexic people. However, quotes from the "famous dyslexics" make it clear that not one of them considered dyslexia a gift. Winston Churchill said "It was not pleasant to feel oneself so completely outclassed and left behind at the beginning of the race." Harry Belafonte recalled being physically abused, because in his school system, children could be whipped for poor schoolwork; Flaubert was described as having wept "giant tears" when the meaning of the letter symbols eluded him.

I show the list of famous dyslexics to David.

"What crap! What does this have to do with me? Well, let me see. I can tell that dyslexia had a lot to do with their achievements. That's obvious."

"Like what?"

"Alexander Graham Bell. No brainer. He had to discover the telephone. He couldn't write a letter. Look! A lot of Army guys. Werner Von Braun, the rocket guy. He just couldn't deal with his anger over not being able to read. Who's this guy? Rodin? Isn't that the movie monster?"

"No, that's Rodan."

"Washington on the Delaware. Maybe he didn't know the right direction. Winston Churchill. Nothing to fear but fear itself. Well, he already knew fear. They probably made him read out loud in class."

David's point is well taken. In the right circumstances, a child can adjust to the inevitable trauma of not being able to read by mobilizing other abilities. Sometimes, these compensations lead to tremendous achievements, the narcissistic wound of the dyslexia pushing the need to succeed. David's ability to see the nuances of color, to experience emotion in such a visceral way, to live in his feelings apart from the language categories we use to wall off experience is quite special.

It's special as an adult. But children are still learning how the world works, trying to sort the new from the already known and given. It's not such a gift then. That's why they need the protection parents offer—a little breathing space until the ability to decode catches up with their intellect.

Do we work to eliminate the gene for dyslexia? Abort fetuses with dyslexia if they can be identified? Or revere dyslexics as a special form of genius? The truth, no doubt, lies somewhere in between, in the space between mothers and children where self-esteem is built.

My time in the library was informative. It was comforting to know I wasn't alone in feeling that living with a learning disabled child is a study in high contrasts and intense hues. But theory is a cold, steel scaffold, an empty building whose rooms still need painting. It was right and all wrong. It still didn't explain David, my fleshy, funny, fresh-mouthed son or why I was still sad, even now that he was reading and I had "proof" he was smart. Why did I care so much anyway? I put my notes away to use for my course at City University on the Psychological Aspects of Learning Disabilities.

This time my answer wasn't going to be found between the pages of a book. Where could I look now for help? Perhaps, as Freud suggested, the path to reality is best found by way of a detour. Just say what comes to mind. . . .

## PART VII

# Bring Me the Broom of the Wicked Witch of the West

*"I never killed anything willingly," Dorothy sobbed, "and even if I wanted to how could I kill the Wicked Witch? If you who are Great and Terrible, cannot kill her yourself, how do you expect me to do it?"*

*"I do not know," said the Head, "but that is my answer, and until the Wicked Witch dies you will not see your uncle and aunt again. Remember that the Witch is Wicked—tremendously Wicked—and ought to be killed. Now, go."*

—L. Frank Baum
The Wizard of Oz 1900

# Chapter 12

# Words and Wondering

In graduate school, I joined the group "professional." I found my clinical voice, a new vocabulary that helped me summarize my findings, classify cases, and maintain my objectivity. A subtle shift. The woman isn't full of despair because she lost her lover, she is "depressed"; the older man who starts shouting and pacing after forgetting what he has said a moment before is "in the early stages of a memory disorder"; that child who talks like a robot is "on the Aspberger's continuum."

I took to the arcane language of psychoanalysis, learning its nuances and memorizing its steady, passionless cadence. I wrote professional papers in all their dry and desiccated purity. Now I am seeing something wrong with this dialect of distant observation; something wrong with me. Before I feel anything, I find a name for it, forming abstract concepts that hold back emotions like a dike.

Suddenly, my language starts to break up, becoming meaningless. I hear the diagnoses that David has been given, "dyslexia, dysgraphia, dysarthric," and I hear the word *dis,* the word my adolescent patients use to name a put-down. My precious words fall apart like parchment in old books, drying and crumbling to dust. Sometimes they rise and burn bright for a moment, July 4th firecrackers in a perfect star pattern, falling invisibly to earth. Or Pauline's string of pearls ripping and rolling away across the floor, one or two gone forever.

Images pour through the spaces left by the lost words. David, learning to ride a bike, his nervous smile and new tallness as he wheels it around, haltingly sure for the first moment that he will be able to ride like other kids. David, uncomfortable in a pizza parlor, me having dragged him to a concert only I wanted to see. David, unable to tell me and asking me for more pizza, more drink, more, more. David, running gracelessly up the hill to catch the school bus. Me, stuck forever in a paroxysm of rage after he has hit Dan, a vise tightening around my chest, screaming words that are as irrevocable as acts.

Simple words take the place of the old ones. SAD. MEAN. MAD. AWFUL. ANGRY.

But it's not all bad. Behind the lost language is a door, an entry into a kingdom of the senses. I hear, smell, see things that never would have entered consciousness. The clink-swoosh sound of the whisk as cream turns to solid in a cold metal bowl, the smell of different bodies on summer streets, my finger pulled fast from the prick of a spiky weed. I am learning a new grammar of memory, with its own rules of order and pleasure.

## Are You My Mother?

Translation:

DAViD S
DEAR MOM
I LOVE YOU BECAUSE YOU ARE NICE TO ME
HAPPY MOTHER'S DAY

Mother's Day Card from David, First Grade

"How are the children, Lissa?" My mother, Pauline, repeats the same question she has asked only moments before.

"They're great. David is doing really well at school. He's reading a lot now."

"Oh good. That's really good, honey. I'm so pleased. It's so important to read. Um . . . I was thinking, honey. How are the children?"

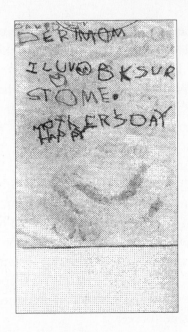

"They are just fine, Mommy. Really good."

"And David. How is David?"

When I talk to my mother on the phone, I pretend she is still herself, ignoring the repetition and the empty formality of her questions. Pauline's reserves of overlearned charm help disguise the harsh realities of the Alzheimer's disease that has brought her to a nursing home in St. Louis. I continue my charade.

"David is great, Mommy. Really."

"He's reading now?"

*What a cheerful liar you are, Lissa. You know they are not really good. David struggles every night with homework, with going to sleep. He's mean to Dan. He hates himself.*

Filling the pause, she adds, "And David, how is he? Is he reading?"

In a way I am lying, but in a way I am not. I am holding fast to an image of Pauline when she still seemed to conquer the world, a picture that can sustain me. My mother is beyond, rising only occasionally from her border world. Memory and perception meld like two superimposed film transparencies; her energy flowing backward toward sleep.

I tell Hillary about the conversation as we drive, too slowly, to the nursing home. She listens with older sister indulgence to my hopeful account. "Yeah, I know," she replies, her voice suddenly tired. "Mommy gives good phone." She has borne the brunt of Pauline's care, visiting her religiously two times a week, balancing the nightmare of finances and insurance. "Don't be frightened. You haven't seen her in a while. She's much worse."

Hillary is brisk and businesslike once she is out of the car.

"Let's go. She doesn't last long." Her mouth tensed, she strides purposefully in front of families visiting patients who can still take pleasure in the warm afternoon sun. Pushing too hard at double doors constructed to give way immediately, we enter into the moldy smell of hallways cleaned of human accidents. A huge sunroom, its glass walls designed to give the illusion of being outside, sports a sad fish tank and plastic palm trees. No decoration can hide the truth—these people are inside, inside, inside forever.

My mother's room is at the end of the hall next to the nursing station. The nurses don't want her frightening other patients when she screams at night, "I'm losing my mind," or rips off her clothes, filled with a nameless horror that has no object, no direction. Her room is an identical pink color to the room Hillary and I shared growing up, the color of babies rooms and nursing homes. There are pictures everywhere. Her wedding. Pauline, elegant in Aunt Mae's borrowed wedding dress and Daddy's swarthy European good looks, his smile showing the gold tooth he later covered. Hillary's wedding and mine. Her and Daddy in Florida, free at last of their immigrant self-consciousness. Her fleshy parents—Granny Annie, Grandpa Morris. All she has left in the world to help her remember.

Pauline is staring at the ceiling as she lies on her bed. Her wiry gray hair, thin as her memory, is carelessly brushed off her face. Her eyelid droops, palsied over one eye, and she stares, accusatorial, with the other. To me, she is still beautiful, a wizened old lioness.

Hillary says, "Look who I brought you, Pauline."

Pauline looks confused, pupils momentarily wide like Dave and Dan when they were babies, but her eyes show no expectation or desire. The light behind them is dim, dimmer, and empty. Pauline raises a hand deformed by arthritis to my face. All through my childhood, she stroked my face to calm my upset over a lost tooth, over a lost love. I take her hand in mine. Today she does not grab it away in irritation.

"How do you like your new room Ma?"

"I don't know honey. It's okay. It just doesn't have the same mien as my old one. That's—M-I-E-N not the other—that's M-E-A-N."

*Can she really still be telling me to spell it correctly? Even with Alzheimer's? Always the teacher. Still the assistant principal of Francis Lewis High School. Nothing matters but education. No wonder I can't handle David. Spell it right. Look it up in the dictionary. All she ever cared about. Pauline, magical and petty in equal measure.*

I take down the pictures, picking one of her father. "Yes, Poppa," she says, pleased at her recognition. "Poppa loved women. He and Momma only spoke Yiddish. They didn't have a pot to piss in."

"Here's you, Mommy. You were so beautiful in that blue satin dress. Daddy loved you to wear that dress."

I lie next to her, stroking her hair. Who will touch her anymore? My mother held me on her hip while she made peach jam from the peaches we picked at the farm next door to the cottage we rented on Mohegan Lake. It's gone now.

I take the Hershey's Kisses from their cheap glass bowl, afterward carefully ironing the creases out of their silver foil wrappers with my thumbnail and folding them neatly. Hillary, brusque, is fixing things around Mommy's room, calling her "Pauline" in clipped, efficient tones or staring listlessly at the fashion magazines and jewelry catalogues Mommy keeps. The corners of their pages are soiled and curled from being looked at idly and again with no recall of having seen them before. My mother catches Hillary looking through *Vogue*. "Oh, those magazines are so stupid," Pauline says, recapturing for a moment her intellectual superiority.

Pauline stares at a picture of me and Hillary I am holding in front of her.

"Miss," she says, addressing me, "these are my daughters." She points to the picture with pride. "Have you met them yet?"

"Oh . . . God," Hillary sighs. "Did you hear that the same way I did?" A giggle slips past my lips.

My mother looks confused. A long time passes in these seconds.

*Its okay, Lissa. That woman isn't Mommy. Mommy is the one who always protects you; she makes the worry go away. She's the fierce one, the one everyone was afraid of. That woman is just a shell, a representative of Mommy.*

I calm myself with fiction. Small islands of safety emerge, a receding tide already washing away the last dizzying moment. I flip through the scrapbook of my memory.

*Pauline says to the other mothers in the playgroup, "Lissa will talk when she is ready." She tells me, "Lissa, you are my very best Scrabble partner." I am eight years old, but I believe her. Pauline, all dreams and remnants, standing in the kitchen, her apron fastened with rhinestone buttons, her French knot unwinding as she puts the tasteless casserole in the oven. She reads me* The Highwayman, *and I dream of passionate love. I don't know we are not rich.*

I retreat into my summary language, trying to form a safe moat of words around my feelings. But there is no escape from the thought. *This will happen to me, too.* There will come a time when I won't recognize my children. My mother's strong, individual face is fading into the generic look of death. She exists only in me, in my memory of her.

*How will David remember me?* The everyday moments I've chosen surprise me. Mommy's fierce defense, her pleasure in me, her awful cooking that we ate every day at the Formica table. Nothing dramatic.

I have missed something, caring only about school, whether he would read, be smart, be me. Will he remember how we laughed together? Think that I loved him the way he was? I call David from the plane going back to New York.

"Do I have what Granny Pauline has?" David asks. "That Altheimer's disease? I forget a lot of things, too." He is afraid.

"No, no of course not. It's different. You are just right. Just the right child for me."

When I get home, David is already asleep. I sit by the edge of his bed, arranging his covers as if that alone could protect him, watching and smelling his still-a-child smell, trying to hold on, understanding for the first time that I will not have him forever.

## PART VIII

# Repeat After Me: There's No Place Like Home, There's No Place Like Home

"Your Silver Shoes will carry you over the desert," replied Glinda. "If you had known their power you could have gone back to your Aunt Em the very first day you came to this country."

"But then I should not have had my wonderful brains!" cried the Scarecrow. "I might have passed my whole life in the farmer's cornfield."

"And I should not have had my lovely heart," said the Tin Woodman. "I might have stood rusted in the forest till the end of the world."

"And I should have lived a coward forever," declared the Lion, "and no beast in all the forest would have had a good word to say to me."

"This is all true," said Dorothy. "But now that each of them has had what he most desired . . . I think I should like to go back to Kansas."

—L. Frank Baum
The Wizard of Oz 1900

# Chapter 13

# Homework, Again

The big hand is on the 12 and the little hand is on the 11—at night. Every delaying technique exhausted, we are now settling down to the math homework. After months of tears and timed drills, multiplication is mastered, but David didn't put the same effort into memorizing addition facts. He still counts on his fingers to add and subtract.

"21–7? Does it equal 12?"

"Try again Dave."

"Thirteen?" David looks at me with raised eyebrows, hopeful about putting one over. "21–7? Is it 7?" Using a technique he has learned while arguing, David shouts it out at me, not angry, but forceful. Raising his voice at the end of a sentence for emphasis ensures that others know he's not afraid of stating an opinion. He knows he's faking this time.

"Oh God, David. Get a grip. Get ahold of yourself. Could it be 13? I'm not ready for prime time, right Lissa? I could do it, I just don't want to take the time to figure it out right. It's easier to get you to do it."

\* \* \*

What's this in your homework book, David? "D-E-A-R 30 minutes?" January of fourth grade. I see D E A R is on every page since September.

"Oh . . . it means drop everything and read."

"I haven't ever seen you drop anything and read. You haven't been doing that."

"I read a lot at school. I always read with Mrs. Greene. We always do reading."

"What happened to the other nights in the week? The four that you don't see Mrs. Greene? How about from now on no TV until D-E-A-R is D-O-N-E ?"

"We read a lot at our special program. We read a lot about science and I read with my friends. "We try to look up wicked words in other languages in Dad's dictionaries."

"Not what I had in mind, D-E-A-R. And not what your teacher had in mind, either."

"Look, Lissa. We've just gotten off on the wrong foot about this. Let's get on the right foot. It doesn't mean Drop Everything and Read. It means Do Erase Anything Written."

"Do you think I was born yesterday?"

"It means Do Erase Anything Read. No? No good? Lissa. You have to trust me. C'mon Lissa. Have a little faith." David furrows his brows in concern for my welfare.


I'm proud that David knows the importance of limits—as long as they are not being imposed on him.

"You're spoiling Dan. You still treat him like he's in kindergarten. He needs to toughen up. He doesn't always need an extra donut at Bella's. He has to learn the meaning of the word *no*."

In Ray's Pizza, David goes berserk that Dan wants the same meat pie he was getting.

"D-a-a-n, you don't even like meat, you don't like hamburgers, and you won't like that. Dan doesn't want a meat pie. He'd rather have lasagna."

"David, please stop this." Practically begging, I'm so tired of feeling angry at him for this kind of stuff. Rather than make a scene in front of strangers, I buy David an extra meat pie and get us out of there. In the privacy of the car, tightlipped, I ask, "David, what was that about?"

"I don't know, Mommy. I get jealous. I can't help myself. I don't want Dan to have anything."

"Even if it's the same as yours? There was enough for both of you."

"Even if we have exactly the same thing. He has to have something I don't want. That's the only thing I feel is fair."

A stunning insight. What's not fair? Can we bear to say it out loud? It's not fair that he has this. This learning disability, this dyslexia, this dysgraphia, this trouble finding words. It's not fair that he wanted to learn to read and that it was so hard for him, that he really tried and all his trying couldn't make it all right. It's true. That's not fair. That he should want so badly to play sports and be good in gym and it's still impossible. That he should have to face humiliation. It's true, that's not fair.

Wait a minute. He's also really bright. He can think faster than many other children his age. He has parents who (most of the time) love him. He can get the help he needs. Others have it far worse. So he has to struggle a little more with some things. So what?

Later that week, David wants to dictate his writing homework, because the physical act of writing is hard. I've discussed it with Mrs. Greene, and she feels refusing would give David some incentive to learn to type.

"It's so not fair to me, Lissa. It's always hard for me to write. The other kids' parents write it for them, and it's not even that hard. It's not fair."

"Life is not fair, David."

David moves in for the kill. "You, Lissa, you are the witch who made it unfair."


As we snorkel closer to the reef, David grabs onto my neck, terrified. "No Lissa, no. There's a barracuda in the water. I saw it last year. The fish are poisonous. I can't go. I won't look." It's a long way to swim back for nothing.

"Hold my hand, David. I won't let you get hurt. You won't be so afraid." I'm bluffing, but maybe he can use the belief to try with me what he won't try alone. We re-form, a floating funny quadriped. Toody and Muldoon, Mutt and Jeff, swimming together, breathing in unison. At first, David grabs tightly, later with diminishing fear. Luminous yellow, iridescent blue, deep purple fishes, and pink anemones offer their seductive freedom. He drops my hand.

Back on land, he says, "It's not so scary."

## Processing Phunny

"I love vampires."

David, already half-asleep from our before-bed reading ritual, catches the phrase and bolts upright. "Do you really love vampires, Mom?"

"No, it's the character talking in the book we're supposed to be reading together. I don't have any personal interest in them."

He continues, clearly excited. "Do the vampires like garlic? I see you don't like garlic. Why don't you like garlic? Is Dracula kind of bald? Does he wear a cape like Batman? Except he kind of hunches over?"

"David, do you mean Nosferatu? He was a famous Dracula."

"They showed this old movie on 'Are You Afraid of the Dark.' The Dracula was scary. Tell me more about Nosferogers, Mom."

"No," I correct him again, "He's called Nosferatu."

"Yeah, tell me all about Nosferogers."

"It's *not* Nosferogers." It takes me a while to realize he's made a combination of Nosferatu and Mr. Rogers, the children's TV show host.

David makes combinations like Nosferogers partly because he's anomic and can't remember the proper name so easily. Floating around it in the temporal lobe, the names join other sounds, but not any random sound. His choice of the specific combinations are often emotionally determined, his fantasies flowing in to fill the gaps in the cognitive wiring. Despite my mostly benevolent behavior, David is sometimes afraid of me, worried that I'm not who I appear. He, too, is a horrifically good child at school, a real "best behaved," while underneath feeling angry. He selects Rogers and not some other name, because Rogers is monstrously benign, a perfect foil for Dracula.

His subsequent talk confirms my interpretation. "What if Mr. Rogers were really a vampire? That would be funny. He could just be fooling people being so nice. Maybe being nice is just a way he has of hiding his true identity."

David continues, pretending to be Mr. Rogers on his show. " 'Oh it's a beautiful day in the neighborhood. But it's a little too sunny in here for me. I'll just keep my sunglasses on. Oh, look, here comes the Postman.'

" 'Hello Mr. Rogers. Why are you wearing sunglasses?'

" 'Why don't you just come in the back with me, Mr. Postman, and I'll show you.' " David turns, his teeth bared.

No question, David is *phunny*, our name for when the wrong word jumps out of his mouth, those times when a malapropism slips past the guardians of self-observation. Word nonsense. Phunny is when you weren't actually planning to be humorous.

Another day: Three Tuskegee Airmen are hanging off the G.I. Joe helicopter with one hand. A soldier lying on a stretcher stares impassively, accepting his fate while a medic attends to him; another Joe is rigged with his arm poised to pull the rip cord of his parachute. Down below, the Desert Storm vehicle cruises. The Joes on the ground are feeling a lot of pressure. They're under siege. Their sargent is lining them up, yelling at them for their lack of discipline, telling them they are not good recruits. David, still resenting me for having come down hard on him for a sloppy book report, is *very* sympathetic to the new Joes.

"Sometimes that Army sergeant is no better than the Gazpacho."

"David, do you mean the Gestapo?"

"Yeah, isn't that what I said? That's what I said. What did I call them? The Gazpacho? What is Gazpacho, anyway? I know I've heard that before."

"It's the Italian summer soup I let you taste at the restaurant."

"Oh . . . Well maybe it was part of a secret Axis plan to poison the Allied Forces. Never give in. Fight the Gazpacho, Mom."

Maybe the fact that he is *phunny* is one reason why David became so *funny*. It was a way of mastering something he couldn't control.

Something that is experienced passively can be traumatic. Something you create on purpose is a lot better. Now if people will laugh, he has made it happen. The joke will not be at his expense. The laughter brings a warm rush of acceptance, of admiration.

But in the end, he's *really* funny. His ability to laugh at his own pretensions makes his other irksome behavior lovable, or at least forgivable. At a recent party, David, seated with the other kids, was miffed because a waiter wouldn't let him order from the adult menu. Adamantly refusing the pedestrian hamburger, he wanted stuffed lobster.

"Why didn't that guy take my order?" David looks genuinely puzzled.

"Maybe because you are a child."

With impeccable timing, David bends on one knee, grabs my arms, and throws his head slightly back. "Say it isn't so, Lissa. Just please, say it isn't so."

A table of grown-ups are laughing with him, admiring his ability to dramatize his predicament—an adult palate stuck in a child's body, waiting for time to catch up with him, forced to make due with chopped meat. Funny is his, now.

## Lessons from the Fourth Grade

Things are much better in fourth grade. I'm more used to doing the homework now, and I can do most of it. I'm doing good in fourth grade. I'm going to move to a higher math group. I got a little medal for having mastered my multiplication facts. But I still try to add on my fingers.

In second and third grade, I learned a lot of different ways to put off doing the homework. Here are some of my suggestions for kids who are still in third and second grade. They worked for me. Add some of your own!

SOME WAYS TO AVOID YOUR HOMEWORK

All my suggestions distract the people who are trying to make you do your homework. You can avoid your homework without even lying or refusing to do it. You can

avoid your homework and not get punished. It's true. Forgetting your homework book or lying about what you have
to do is not a good idea. You will always get caught, and
people will get really angry at you because you've lied.
Then you know what you are in for—a talk. How I hate
every time Mom says we have to *talk* about something.
Whenever she says it, I have to try real hard to try and
think about something else until it's over. I try not to hear,
because it makes me feel bad. So try these ways instead.

1. Start a fight with your brother. This is sure-fire!
Everyone gets mad at you, but by the time it's straight-
ened out, at least a half hour will have gone by. Everyone
will yell at you about how mean you are to your brother,
but they will not make you feel bad by saying that you
spelled "read" as "red" again.

2. When your mother comes toward you with the homework, say, "I really have to go to the bathroom right
now." Close the door. Take your time. If you're lucky,
she'll get busy with something else and forget about you.

3. Say, "I'm hungry. Get me some food right now." If she
refuses, say, "I am really starving. I didn't get a chance
to eat lunch today." Or, even better, "You didn't give me
anything I liked for lunch."

4. Ask them a question that has nothing to do with the
homework, like, "I have been wondering. How many
bones does a human have in its body?" It is very, very
good if it's a question that they don't immediately know
the answer to. Say, "Maybe we could look it up in the encyclopedia." Parents love to help you learn things.

5. Figure out what your parents are really interested in.
Do they like your drawings? Start drawing. Do they like
you to be curious about things? Now is a good time to ask
questions. This works best if there's something your mom
or dad want to show you or teach you about. For example,
my dad loves rock and roll. He's always getting these videos from the video store on the history of rock and roll.

Homework time is an especially good opportunity to offer Dad some alone time with you. Maybe you should watch that video he got out. When I tried this, Dad had no clue. I thought Mommy would hit the ceiling. She kept yelling, "Larry, he has to do his homework! What are you doing?" She didn't yell at me, though. She yelled at Dad.

6. Say, "This is too hard for me. Can you help me?" It probably is too hard for you, anyway. How can Mommy help you? Can she write down the words if you tell her what to say? Can she just correct the spelling mistakes for you? Can she type the homework on the computer? Tell her that the parents of lots of the other kids in your class do that for them. Throw in names of kids she knows. It's better if you say, "Jonah's mom does that for him," not just "All the kids' moms do it." Be sure to say that your teacher said it was okay.

7. Be sad. They know things are hard for you. Get them to do as much as you can. You know it's important to them that you do well. This can be useful. Even kids without problems can get their parents to do their homework, because parents want your work to look better. Even Mommy says that most of the book report posters were done by the mothers.

8. Make the most of the fact that they want you to like school. Bargain. For example, "If I do my spelling homework before 8 o'clock, can I watch The History Channel?" Make a deal. Try, "If I do my homework without complaining all week, can I get a toy on Friday with Dad?" Never, never, do your homework for nothing.

9. If your brother is watching TV, even if you've been forbidden to watch TV before your homework, go in and watch with him. Say, "He had it on, it's not my fault."

10. Say you have no pencils. Get new pencils. Sharpen them carefully. Sharpen them again. Dump out the fillings. Arrange your erasers on the table. Drop your pencil. It broke its point. You have to start all over.

## Why Read?

It helps when you read a book to imagine what the characters look like. It helps you understand and remember what's going on in the book. Otherwise, it's just a lot of words that slip right out of your head. I think I started to see the books like that when I was in second grade, when we started to read books that didn't have a lot of pictures anymore. I would pretend that the people were people that I had seen on TV shows. I read this book in school, *Shiloh*, and I imagined Marty's father was somebody from the TV show *For Your Love.* I think a boy in a *Dear American* book is Josh Ford in the TV show *Popular.* For a long time, I didn't like to read, and I would see these characters a lot on TV, so I used them because I knew what their faces looked like. Once I used a kid I knew from my camp as the brother of the main character in a *Goosebumps* book, because they kind of had the same whiney personality. I don't have to imagine anything when I read the books on war, because they aren't stories, and they have their own pictures. I look at the pictures to see what the tanks look like or what uniforms the soldiers wore. I read those for information. I know more about the different wars and the battles than any other kid on my bus. Nobody can believe how much I know.

We had to write for school on what we would rather do, curl up with a book or play with the computer. To tell the truth, I really wouldn't do either, but if I had to choose, I would read a book. I'm really bad at computer games, so I'd much rather read a book. At computer games, I can't press the button fast enough in a shooting game and I forget how to log in. I'm scared in fifth grade we'll have to do a lot of work on the computer and I won't remember how to log in. When you read you can learn things, but on the computer games, they are mostly shooting and you are pressing all these buttons and you get confused and mad and yell. But if you are reading a book and you can't read a word, you can ask someone and the book doesn't shut off. When you are reading, you can sit on your couch and relax and forget about everything. That is the most important thing. It can calm you down. When I am in the car and I want to read a book, I can tell everyone to be quiet so I can concentrate on reading. When you are on a computer game, you can get tense. I'd still rather watch TV than do either, but I see what Mommy means when she says that reading can take you away from your worries for a while. And sometimes the TV is stupid. Like in the morning, I like to watch the news. But they don't really tell you the news so much as make jokes about each other and talk about their hair. So sometimes it's better to read the newspaper because then you can just see what is going on.

I always liked to make up stories with my G.I. Joes or with my other toys. Sometimes I would get so wound up in the stories that when Mommy called me to go to dinner, I would hear her, but I wouldn't really be listening. The game was much more important. Mommy would sometimes yell when I was playing a game where everyone got killed and there was a lot of shooting. She'd say, "I just can't stand these games. They make me nervous." I always knew it was a game, not real. What was wrong with her? I always knew it was imagination. Did she think I didn't know the difference? But it still felt really important, like I had to finish the game more than I had to go to dinner or to listen to Mommy. Now I feel the same way when I read. It's like a game I'm making up as I read, especially if I read a war story. I read one about Confederate soldiers. I could see the soldiers and the way I would set them up. I imagine the guys falling, "Aargh," when they are shot. I hear them saying things like, "You will die now." I think about why they would do things, like run up a hill or if they are really scared. What if feels like to be so scared that you can't stand it anymore or if they are hurt and really bloody. I never stop in the middle of a chapter. I want to finish the book. I try to read fast, and I always measure how thick the book I'm reading is. The new *Harry Potter* book is 710 pages. That will be the longest book I've ever read. Mommy says it doesn't matter if you read fast. She doesn't read fast, but she reads more than most people do. But I always count the number of pages I have read and see if I can do it faster. Mommy keeps saying over and over that when you read it's like writing your own story. I say, "I know, Mom." It's annoying when she keeps saying it. I do know what she means. I'd like to be a writer. Mommy says that it's easy, you can just write down the pictures you see in your mind. I have always seen lots of pictures in my mind, but I don't like to write the letters and I don't know how to type yet. Sometimes I will tell them to Mommy and she writes them down for me. I guess it's just stories like I used to do with the G.I. Joes.

I still like books that give me information. But I like scary books, too, like *Goosebumps.* But they always end the chapters the same way. Like something terrible is going to happen, but by the next chapter it all works out and you were scared for nothing. Sometimes that's annoying.

I read on the bus going to camp because there's no one my age on the bus. Jonah goes on another bus, and I won't talk to Dan. So I bring a book every day. They said we have to read every day between fourth and fifth grade and at first I was so mad that I yelled at my tutor. I said I never want to see her again because I had to read anyway. I told her to go away. But now I write down every day the name of the book I read and the date I started it and finished it. At first I just read easy books, like books for third graders, like *Secrets of the Bog* and *Alien Invasion* and *Mummies.* I figured I could get a lot of books on the list that way. Now I'm reading *Goosebumps,* and soon I'm going to start a young *Indiana Jones* book. Mom says it's better to read a harder book slow because it's more interesting, but I'm not sure yet. But it does make me feel less lonely on the bus. I used to just sleep because there was nothing to do. Now I make sure I pack my book every day. Sometimes I just skim. I skimmed *The Invisible Man* by H. G. Wells because I wanted to know what happened in the end before I had to read the whole book. I just got the new *Harry Potter* book. I already read the first two, and I'm on the third one. I read the first one in school, but I'm going to buy it anyway so I can have them as a set to give to my own children or keep them until they are worth something. I like to collect books and have a lot of them on my shelves. Even if I never read them.

Why read? 'Cause you can make your own world. And it's like having a friend, if it's a good book that can keep your interest. And there is stuff you can't learn about even on The History Channel or the Discovery Channel. I guess that it is sometimes worth it to go through all those words—but only sometimes, if there's something you really want to learn about. I hate it when it's a dumb book. Then I won't even look at it.

## Home from School

It's 2:50, time to meet David at the bus. He likes me to meet him. He just won't admit it.

He dawdles getting off, as usual the last one to come down the steps. How does Joe the bus driver stand it day after day? He's dressed in his favorite long, loose pants, the ones that make him feel like a rap star, size 14 on a 10-year-old boy. He's got his Grandpa Ray's World War II dog tags around his neck and John Lennon sunglasses (a left-over from a "Wild West" promotional giveaway at Burger King), back-pack slung rebelliously over one shoulder. It's a look. Like Larry says—David is a true original. His shoes are untied—still. He can tie them, but now he chooses not to. Some god must protect him, because miraculously, he doesn't trip over the laces anymore. He'll come in, throw the backpack on the kitchen table, and head directly into the family room to try and watch TV before doing his homework. When I turn off the TV, he'll try and get me to do a little more of the homework than I should. Maybe just copy over his Wordly Wise definitions or write the answers to his book report questions. I'll lose my temper. Quarreling is part of our love song, forgiveness our chorus. We'll struggle, but not too hard. He'll do the homework himself, but not before he's struck a good deal for the dinner of his choice.

"Yo" he says when he sees me, pointing his fingers downward like Puff Daddy and managing to look as much like Puff Daddy as any white ten-year-old possibly could. He doesn't want me to walk next to him. That would be babyish.

I look at him with wonder. I know now this is the child I was meant to have.

**PART IX**

Postscripts

# Chapter 14

# Lessons Learned

If others read in our experience a tale of triumph, a more truthful depiction might be that each night we went to sleep and every morning we woke up. No angel Gabriel flew in the window to choose us; no one offered us ruby slippers; no wars were won. While the weeds with their vital underground root life never left our garden, we found landscape fabric that would slow their progress. When we stopped lying to ourselves, ways to cope emerged. What was traumatic became prosaic, joining an associative web and becoming "our life." We learned to laugh, we let the Painted Ladies go, and we found words for our stories. We became a little funnier and a little meaner than before.

Sometimes a mother who watches and listens can learn things that professionals fail to see. Given all we did wrong, our story reads more like a "who-dun-it" than a "how-to" book. We did learn a few things, so I made a list. The list seems simple—so mom-and-pop, so unprofessional. But Dr. Weinstein or Lissa Siever, Glinda or the Wicked Witch, it's what I wished I'd known before starting. It's broken down into sections, because when I needed this advice, I was usually too upset to focus on a lot of information at once.

## Getting Evaluated

- **When? Don't wait and see.** If your gut tells you something feels different about your child, check it out now. It's easier to know that your child needs to be evaluated if he's not speaking in three-word sentences by age three or seems much clumsier than his peers. However, processing problems, early on, can also present as social phenomena—the child who's afraid to go to the playground because it's too busy, the child who hates birthday parties or panics at any new experience, the child who is overly ritualized and has to sit in the same seat in nursery school every day. **Don't wait**—it's time to find out. Mothers have an intuitive awareness of behavior that doesn't follow the usual developmental trajectory. Seriously avoidant behavior (i.e., won't look at the letters) is often a sign of an undetected learning problem. There's no downside to getting your child tested. But there is a serious risk in waiting until your child hates school.

- **Who should do it?** Your child should be evaluated by a trained neuropsychologist or a clinical psychologist with a specialization in learning disabilities. Of course, you'll hate/mistrust the person who tests your child if they bring bad news. At least be sure you can trust their professional qualifications. Reading problems of disparate origin might look the same on the surface. **There is no one dyslexic child.** A remediation program must be based on an understanding of the underlying processing issues. A good evaluation should do more than document your child's problems. It should tell you how the child can learn and offer the most profitable routes to remediating the problem. For example, some children have an easier time taking in information through the visual channel or need a lot of motor involvement in order to remember.

## Getting Help

- **Don't listen to those voices in your head telling you not to do anything.** No one wants their child to have problems. It's a harder life. So it's natural to pretend that it's not happening. This pretending takes classic forms:

I'll just wait and see—the school says to wait until after second grade.

My child isn't interested in reading. He likes sports.

Getting help will make him feel different.

Don't give in to these impulses.

• **Intervene early.** The research is clear: Earlier is better. The ideal time to start a remediation program is between four and seven years. One consequence of delayed identification is that it occurs late in the child's cognitive and linguistic development, so one might already be pushing the edge of his cognitive flexibility and ability to learn skills. Ten years has been suggested as a breaking point, because there are marked changes in spatial pattern recognition, Braille, and map reading. Others cite puberty as setting limits on language development.

Second, what child would like to continue trying to do something that makes him feel stupid? The more you wait, the more he avoids. There's less social stigma for the child in getting help early.

Third, your child already knows something is wrong, even if he doesn't have a name for it. Children fear it's something far worse than a reading problem. Offer help, not false protection. I could not have guessed how early David was aware of his difficulty and how obsessed he was with reading at the same time that he found it impossible. His overtly dismissive attitude covered his pain at being different. Behavior that appeared "lazy" and "disinterested" masked frustrated desires to learn. Did your child want to talk? To walk? It's likely he wants to read, too.

• **Don't tutor your child yourself.** Even if you know what you are doing. A child can get another tutor; he can't get another parent. When he sees the anxious look in your eyes when he doesn't "get it," it only makes him want to avoid reading even more.

- **Choose a tutor with specific training in reading remediation.**
A reading remediation tutor is not a homework helper or a
teacher from your child's school who will more carefully review
classroom material. Dyslexic children need to be taught a different way, using a multisensory remediation program, best offered in a one-on-one setting. The best-researched ones are
based on the Orton Gilligham Method or the Lindamood Bell
system. You wouldn't get your car repaired by a salesman on
the lot; you'd insist on a mechanic. Your child deserves as
much.

- **A tutor must understand the dynamic context of learning.**
Usually, the mastery of an adult skill is a source of intense
pleasure for a child. Think of catching a baseball or riding a
bike. For a dyslexic child, however, learning to decode is a
painful frustration. He will try to avoid the anxiety that inevitably accompanies his efforts. A tutor must help the child join
an enterprise where the child's vulnerability will be exposed.
Like a therapist, they have to deal with the child's resistance to
learning and act as a scaffold, providing structure and support
as well as information. In the beginning, before there are suc-
cesses to look back on, the child's desire to try comes from the
attachment to their tutor and from a feeling of acceptance and
safety.

- **Choose a tutor *you* trust.** A good tutor is part of your life
as well as your child's life. To face a disability is hard; if your
child feels you don't trust his tutor, he will exploit your un-
happiness in order to avoid a difficult, painful task. You and
the tutor must be able to stand united and demonstrate to the
child that you really want him to continue, despite the hard-
ships.

## What You Can Do

- **Trust your child's passions. Lean on them.** This is the *single
most important lesson.* It was a surprise to me that the activities
David appeared to use to avoid reading included attempts to

compensate for his difficulties. Playing helped him manage the trauma of being unable to read by transforming reality in the service of mastery. By relying on his passions, he borrowed the energy to overcome anxiety. The dinosaurs helped him hook up letters and sounds; the maps helped him write, the G.I. Joes helped him remember names and temporal sequences. David had a tremendous drive to learn, but he couldn't take in information the way it was taught in school.

• **Let them play. Play is a powerful tool that can be harnessed in the service of learning.** For all children, play makes the world smaller, changing what had been experienced passively into something chosen, something owned. Feelings of helplessness are gradually worn away. David's games allowed him to feel powerful; by identifying with the Joes, in fantasy he could transcend the limitations of his disability. Play, because it is pleasurable, allows the child to generate enough repetition to reliably internalize new information. The repetition supports the development of automaticity at the same time that the decreased anxiety leaves more energy for learning. For children with cognitive difficulties, play creates a potential space where they are free to learn without being humiliated. Play is their passion, a passion that will eventually transfer to their love of reading, which must connect with their emotional life if it is to transcend the narrow mission of decoding.

• **Don't *just* talk to your child. Get down on the floor and play with them.** Not just if your child is dyslexic. Forget experts. Children's play is a language. If you learn to speak it, you'll know how to make the critical decisions. Then talk to your child. When I first started writing with David, I thought he was unusually articulate about his difficulties. When I started to talk more directly to the children I saw for evaluation, I was surprised how many of them could be equally forthcoming about their difficulties. Perhaps we, as parents, shut them up. It's an old axiom of therapy that problems that can be put into words will be less malignant.

• **Read to your child while he looks at the words. Read to your child more.** *Don't* make him read to you. He will—when he can. Reading to your child is important for two reasons. First, he comes to associate reading with a safe, secure, and pleasurable relationship. Second, hearing the word read to him acts as a kind of priming. Prior exposure to words, shapes, or sounds facilitates the subsequent identification of them from cues or fragments, upping the likelihood that your child will be able to recognize the word when he sees it.

• **Become a learning partner, not a tutor.** Read the books your child is reading. Get videos of the books to help him get to know the characters. Learning disabled children often have a hard time "entering" a book because they have trouble remembering the character names. If the initial entry into a book is hard, they put it down. Previewing the book, making a chart of the names, or watching a video all help.

• **Provide a predictable, stable environment with a lot of repetition.** Because it's harder for dyslexic children to use language to mediate their emotional states and arousal, they often feel overwhelmed by new situations. Familiarity is a strong preference. Repetition aids the sense of familiarity and safety. It also helps them discriminate signal from noise. If there's a lot of variance in a signal, it's harder to understand what's normal. This pattern is true both in learning phonemic discrimination, but also in being able to understand what their parents want from them.

• **Get support.** Maybe this means joining a support group of mothers of learning disabled children, or going into therapy, or calling your mother every day until she starts to leave the answering machine on—anything that makes you feel less alone. Ultimately, getting yourself support will help your child, because he needs you to act as an auxiliary ego. The diagnosis is a trauma for both parent and child, because the meaning of having a child with difficulty is usually hiding in an obscure corner of the parent's early development. If you find yourself needing to hide your child's difficulties, it's time to look further. Therapy can help hasten the mourning process that must take place before the parent can advocate for their child's needs. Before a parent can fight for her child—fully—she has to move beyond a denial of the child's difficulties, mourn a fantasy of the perfect child, and simultaneously accept and detach from the child's struggles.

The child might also need therapy to learn to encapsulate the learning problems, so that the sense of failure does not spread to a more global self-assessment. Also, the learning problems do bring on other social problems and difficulties with the inevitable increased anger.

• **Advocate shamelessly for your child.** After you've done everything else, worked out your own problems, and supported your child, fight for him. No one cares about your child as much as you. You have to educate yourself about the problems, and if you can't fight well yourself, hire a professional to make sure the school provides what is needed. If the school can't offer what's needed, it's your right to have the school system pay to have your child educated in a special school for learning disabled children.

## Life Lessons

• **You can't control everything.** Sometimes they have to struggle on their own. It can be hard to decide when to give help. However, it's a short step to doing things for them—a step that might ultimately make them feel more hopeless and defective. Perhaps a good rule of thumb is to attempt to contain the partnership to areas of school learning and to give a gentle prod toward independence in other areas where their anxiety can be reduced enough to offer them mastery of new experiences.

• **Anger is inevitable. It's a harder and more complicated job, for you and for your child. You might be better at it than you think.** I imagined that David would be better off with a mother who never got angry. Surprisingly, recognizing my own anger helped David see that he didn't have to falsely cover his own rage and jealousy. He didn't have to feel like an oddball for being so mad. No candidates for sainthood, we developed strategies to heal after a particularly rough night of blame and disappointment. We repair our relationship when it breaks, learning slowly that anger doesn't destroy love and that eventually love will tame anger. Far, far from perfect, but "good enough."

• **Keep your eyes on the prize. Reading is only one part of life.** This is a funny thing to say after having written a whole book on learning to read. However, decisions about schooling have to be made in the larger context of your child's life—of making friends, of building self-esteem, and of his extended struggle to become his own person. We thought our job was to get him to read, but our real triumph was learning to laugh.

• **Embrace your limits. Through them, new possibilities will emerge.** I never would have wished for David to be dyslexic. It didn't make him a better person or me a better mother; it made us different, forcing us to grow in ways we hadn't anticipated. His difficulties also offered me a chance to have a deeply intimate relationship with my son; one I might not otherwise have had. Paradoxically, having a learning disability was the source of David's resilience. A great self-observer, he has an uncanny awareness of how his mind works. Because the language of a dyslexic child is less "seamless," there is a more permeable membrane between consciousness and those processes usually shut off from awareness. Just as he becomes exquisitely sensitive to the subprocesses and routines that go into breaking the code of the written word, he is alert to other aspects of his cognitive and emotional functioning. These developed strengths remain, functionally independent of their original source in his fear of humiliation. David is also a fine writer; his access to visual material and imagery gives his words a directness that my own lack.

## What I Learned

What would I say to kids who were having trouble reading? I'd say "Sit down and shut up. It's tough to be you." No, just kidding. I'd say be sure to tell your parents that you are having a problem, because you will definitely know you can't read before they do. They won't know unless you tell them, but they are the only ones that can get you help. If you're afraid to tell your parents, you'll end up in late elementary school and the teacher will call on you to read and you won't know how to read a word that you don't already know—like off the top of my head, *xenophobia*. I know what that is—fear of foreigners. Actually, I know that because I had to look it up this morning.

I'd say it seems really terrible to not be able to read when everyone else does, but you *will* be able to read. But you won't just wake up one morning and know how to read. It takes practice and hard work with a tutor. Not being able to read is really not the worst thing in the world. There are things that a lot worse and can't be changed, like being so poor that you are starving or having a really serious disease. Some kids in very poor places like Africa don't even get to go to school, so they never even learn to spell a single word or read at all. You will learn to read; it will just take you a while. I really don't know what to say, but this is about as close as I can come.

Parents should get a tutor and try to work once and a while with their kid. Don't be too nice and let them get away with everything. Be firm. Parents should mostly remind kids that they will learn to read, just like I did, because a kid doesn't know that not being able to read could go away. Don't say, "You will learn to read by third grade." A kid who is not reading will think that is the end of the universe. Say you will learn *soon*. Many famous movie stars like that guy from *The Sopranos* with the red

hair or Winston Churchill and Nelson Rockefeller had dyslexia, and look how good they turned out.

## Permanent Scars

One night, we sat up till 1 in the morning reading over our
book. The next day, Mommy asked how I thought being
dyslexic had changed me. I said we should write about
the things that stayed with me, even though I read now. I
wanted to call it *Permanent Scars.* Mommy didn't like
that title because she said I had done so well and she
wanted the book to give people hope. She suggested *In-
delible Ink* for things you couldn't erase. But I insisted,
because *Permanent Scars* is the way I feel them. In the
end, Mommy agreed, because she said that it was the
truth for me, even if it was hard for her to hear that there
were hurts that she couldn't make go away. So . . . *Permanent Scars.*

What does it mean when you can't read like other kids
do? It means you're a mutant, a freak. When does that
feeling go away? Duh, Mom. When they teach you to read.
Once you learn to read, it's hard to remember what it was
like before. It's too hard to remember not knowing the
letters and what it felt like. I was five when that happened.
I feel like I always knew them now and I always knew
how to read.

By the end of second grade, the first half of the hurdles
had been jumped. I got some reading, some I couldn't get
at all, and my confidence was still shot. By the end of third
grade, the last of the hurdles was being jumped. I had a
bad social year though. By fourth grade, the hurdles were
jumped. It was now life as we know it. I didn't like having
a tutor anymore. I started to hate Mrs. Greene. It made
me feel like I was still stupid, so I told her to go away.

Over the years, the reading problem left some permanent traces. I always felt when I was reading that I

needed stuff like extra toys, and my parents felt sad for me so I always got these extra toys that I didn't really need. Mommy Lissa, for sure, never knew how to say no to me. I guess I'll always prefer TV a little bit to reading because it's so much easier. I still have to really want to read something. I'll always have the scar of that one teacher who didn't understand the kid with a problem, and I still feel very bad if a teacher yells at me for being slow at something, like typing. Then I won't want to go to school the next day.

I'll always wonder why words don't sound like they are spelled. Like why should Home Depot be pronounced *deepo* and not *dep-pot,* or why is colonel said like *kernel* and not *col-low-nel*, or why is knight not *kuh-nite?* I could go on.

I still don't like new situations, but once I'm used to things, I'm very good. Like if I can't get a math problem, I still scream, "Lissa, I need help!" and put it off till 10 o' clock at night. Then I'll shake me head and say, "I don't have a clue," when Mommy Lissa tries to explain it to me. I get so nervous, I just can't hear what she's saying.

Oddly, I'm very good at speaking in front of audiences. I don't read my speech, I memorize it and so I read with a lot of expression and always look right at everybody.

There were these other good things, too, like the very attuned sense of humor that Mommy Lissa and I share. Everyone else thinks we are crazy for the things we think are funny. And no matter how much Mommy and I fight, I know that she loves me. We have had to make up a lot of rules to get along together. Like you can't say someone is stupid, and nothing you say or do to the other person after 10 o' clock at night counts, because that is when Lissa starts to get really mad that I am not going to bed. Lissa punished me the other night, but it was at 10:15, so in the morning I told her that the punishment didn't count.

I got her on a technicality. But Lissa took it well and only gave me a playful shot to the head.

My little brother must feel jealous because I got to write a book with my mother and I feel bad about that. Well, not really. I kind of do. I will always have the extra spurt of attention because I was the first son and had a book written. Many people might think reading this book that we have forgotten the younger brother in the book. Daniel always felt he had to be the good child, never get in trouble, and never try to do anything wrong. He's starting to fight back better now.

When I was in first grade, I couldn't do one thing in my phonics book. But look at me now. I'm a great reader and I never even finished one phonics book. Tell them I learned to read, that reading is really easy, and my writing is getting much better, and I know all the multiplication tables, (well, I've forgotten them a little, but I'll learn them again) and we really don't think about reading much anymore. We think about how much I nag. But today, when Mommy told me I couldn't go for my haircut, I didn't nag. Mommy almost called 911 to say I had been taken over by aliens.

Sometimes I wonder what life would have been like if I didn't have this problem. I will always have the scar of deep down in my heart, feeling somewhat different from the other kids, but that pretty much has been overcome. I guess all kids feel that way about something, like being adopted, or being fat, or not looking the way they want.

# Chapter 15

# Looking Backward

"I knew that Mom wanted to write a book that would help other people. But I never really cared about that. *Not at all.* I thought that maybe we'd make some money. I'd be able to buy more G.I. Joes and nobody could say I had used my allowance money already. I knew that Dad wrote a book; I thought my book could sell more copies. I knew I could do better than him!"

David talks with his characteristic, brash honesty, quick to let me know that he is "not my little boy anymore." I wanted him to say how wonderful it was to write a book together, but he no longer needs to see the world the same way I do. He doesn't think of himself as a "child with problems." Now he's just like every other eleven-year-old—obnoxious, rebellious, and highly opinionated about what constitutes a "cool" haircut. He is fierce in pursuit of his desires. Right now, these tend toward getting more Legos and outwitting Dan. He sees his way clear to becoming a marine biologist, or if that fails, a chef "who does exotic food, like Emeril." Nobody's fool; he'll best his father. If he doesn't always use his intelligence to be the best at school, he excels at logical argument and shows real potential at entrepreneurial manipulation. When he tells his teacher with his special, sly grin that his one real talent is nagging, I'm tempted to believe him.

Six years ago when David was diagnosed dyslexic, I could never have dreamed that my painfully shy, gap-toothed child would turn into a sassy eleven-year-old who would easily outdo me in verbal hand-to-hand combat. I couldn't see a future for him, even though I had been an expert on learning disabled children for more than a decade before having my own. But those children weren't my son. If David was unprepared for dyslexia, I was unprepared for my reactions. We were innocent then, thinking dyslexia was the biggest giant we would have to slay.

I wrote this book because I had to. As a trained psychoanalyst, a field that values privacy to a degree that rivals the Mafia code of silence, I was schooled in the absolute necessity for personal anonymity. My first plan was a scholarly distillation of the literature on development and learning disabilities. My second idea was an Oliver Sacks–type exploration of how David's mind functioned. Did I imagine myself the Alexander Luria of motherhood? But romantic science aside, this "subject" was my son. The depth of his pain and his courageous efforts to face the everyday trauma of school revealed the shallowness of both plans. To not speak of personal realities in this context would be cowardice. Like David, who often felt set apart by his difficulties, I needed a confederate to share my experience. Being an "expert" had left me lonely. I couldn't join a support group, I was supposed to be the support. My husband was supportive, but like many fathers, his relationship to the problem was different than mine. He was more rational and separate, and I'm sure he has his own story of this time. I'm grateful that he let me write mine. Writing became my friend, an opportunity to articulate the long journey of a parent of a child with difficulty.

Far more urgent than my own suffering was David's need to talk, to come from behind the wall of silence built around his disability. All people need to tell their stories, yet society still demands that children should be seen and not heard. Outside the context of intensive psychotherapy, children are rarely asked to reflect imaginatively on their experience. It's hard to listen to a child in pain. When it's your own child, when you imagine that you have caused the child's suffering, it's even harder.

If dyslexic children have difficulty forming coherent narratives about the self, I hope this book will offer a record of David's hard work and triumph to refer to when his struggles to read would be over, but the anxieties about learning still remained, as they so often do for dyslexic children.

It is a risky business to write a book with your child. When we started, David was just seven years old. He was eager, even relieved to talk about his problems. By the age of ten, David no longer wanted to focus on his disability. He was reading above grade level, and he wanted his memories to fade into the haven that forgetting offers. So we stopped. Stopped writing anyway, for despite the best compensations, his struggles will be lifelong, showing up in new forms as the demands of his academic life shift. When he was eleven, we reread the book together, adding in details that had been forgotten and laughing over the recorded incidents. I still worry that he will feel betrayed when he rereads the account as a teenager, but I also know how helpful his observations were to me, and could be to other children who do not share his insight and verbal gifts. I didn't want to cause him embarrassment once he was no longer immersed in the experiences described.

The solution was prescribed by the roles we choose. David picked the topics. I asked him questions, and he dictated his answers. Even while knowing strong verbal skills in the context of a disability that affects reading and written language are common, I still find it confusing that a child who can speak as articulately as my son could have a severe learning disability. While putting order to the discussions of various topics, I tried not to change his words. David had veto power over what was written.

"Did you and Davey write a true story, Mom?" Dan asks. At seven, he is concerned with making the all-important distinction between imagination and reality. The reality is that David had a learning disability, diagnosed at age five by "real" scores, IQ scores, reading scores, performances on spelling tests, tests of motor functioning, and assessments of attention. The truth? That's something else, hidden in between how I saw him and the picture he drew of himself. There was no one *real* story.

The far country of childhood is a mystery, lost inevitably in translation to a more mature language. Despite his articulate and moving words, I will never know all of what having a learning disability meant to my son. I will never even know how the letters appeared to him. Too much of any childhood exists in an inchoate form: volcanoes erupting; the teeth of one dinosaur sunk into the flesh of another; the soothing touch of a warm towel after a bath; a special trip to the car wash, the long spaghetti making us laugh as they hit "slap, slap" on the windshield. Which of these precious moments will be chosen to form the central core around which memories organize, melding fantasy and reality, while others are lost?

My son and I wrote a story together, and it was a true story, just as true as the spaces between any mother and child in their funny, private world, as true as any story of childhood can be. We looked for antecedents, and we found consequences. I didn't make him lie and I tried to listen, and in the end that saved us. Telling it helped make our lives whole, allowing us to recapture the pleasure we once felt in just being together before something had to be "fixed." I hope David's courageous words allow other children to give voice to their worries.

# About the Authors

Lissa Weinstein, Ph.D., is an assistant professor in the doctoral program in clinical psychology at City College and The Graduate School of The City University of New York. She is a graduate of the New York Psychoanalytic Institute, currently serves as associate director at the Pacella Parent Infant Center, and is on the adjunct faculty of the Mount Sinai School of Medicine and Columbia Physicians and Surgeons Hospital. She has been working as a clinical psychologist for more than twenty years and has authored numerous articles about developmental psychology for scientific journals as well as contributed to a number of books.

David is a seventh grader in Westchester, New York. He sees himself as a good thinker who knows a lot about geography, dinosaurs, and World War II. He would like to grow up to be a marine biologist, a chef who does fancy food, or a writer—as long as he doesn't have to write the letters himself. He is currently on the honor roll. He would like everyone to know that he is very funny. Today, but not every day, he feels he has an excellent mother.